*"You'll be pleased to hear that it's the Holy Grail.
Have you got it insured?"*

*"Ahh! A hospital bed!
Now I haven't seen
one of these for a
very long time"*

"Isn't that Lovejoy doing a stint on
the Antiques Roadshow?"

MITCHELL BEAZLEY IN ASSOCIATION WITH ARLCS

the Antiques Roadshow

ANTIQUES ROADSHOW

ANTIQUES ROADSHOW

MITCHELL BEAZLEY IN ASSOCIATION WITH ARLCS

the Antiques Roadshow

Foreword **Michael Aspel**

Editor **David Battie**

Fiona Malcolm

Consultants **Paul Atterbury & Hilary Kay**

The Antiques Roadshow
by David Battie and Fiona Malcolm

Previously published as
The Antiques Roadshow: A celebration of the first 21 years
by Fiona Malcolm

First published in Great Britain in 2005 by Mitchell Beazley,
an imprint of Octopus Publishing Group Ltd, 2–4 Heron Quays,
London E14 4JP

ISBN 1 84533 060 9

A CIP record for this book is available
from the British Library

Set in Grotesque MT, Calson 540

Colour reproduction by Fine Arts, HK
Printed and bound in China by
Toppan Printing Company Limited

Senior Executive Editor Anna Sanderson
Executive Art Editor Christine Keilty
Designer Peter Gerrish
Editor Emily Asquith
Copy Editor Emma Clegg
Production Jane Rogers
Special photography Mick Dunning, Tim Ridley,
Nick Goodall, Ron Sutherland

Contents

Foreword

Imagine my delight at being invited to present the *Antiques Roadshow* after so many years as a regular viewer of the programme. My initial euphoria was soon replaced by the enormity of the responsibility I was about to take on. It was, quite simply, a perfect programme, and Hugh Scully had done such a sterling job over many years that I was quite terrified of ruining it.

Now that I'm no longer quite the new boy, I can only say how much of a pleasure and privilege it is to be involved in a programme that is so much a part of British cultural life. I don't think I'm exaggerating when I say that the *Antiques Roadshow* is a broadcasting phenomenon, envied by programme makers the world over.

Who could have predicted that it would be such an instant, uproarious success and that the dynamism of the event could be sustained? And yet it is, because crowds keep coming, still bringing with them some wonderful surprises.

It is, of course, the great British public who make the programme what it is. The day is so intense that I have little time to stand and stare, but when I get a chance to watch the filming on the monitors in the production room, or to mingle with people on the set, I never fail to be amused, entertained and even flabbergasted not only by the objects themselves but by the stories that go with them. I have decided that there can't be a better way to study history than by watching the *Antiques Roadshow*.

I'll always remember the woman who brought along a khaki bag packed with postcards but with a hole in its side. When she invited me to look into the stack of cards, I could see a bullet firmly lodged in the centre. It had been her father's backpack during the Second World War and had saved his life.

Then there was the ring that had belonged to the owner's ancestor during the time of the Great Plague. The ancestor had succumbed to the dreaded disease and been laid out for burial. During the night a servant crept downstairs and tried to steal the ring from her finger, at which moment she miraculously sat bolt upright and no doubt frightened the servant into an early

grave! The "dead" owner of the ring went on to have several children and lived to a ripe old age.

Even after several years on the programme, I'm still astonished and gratified by the patience of the hundreds of people who queue at every Roadshow, sometimes in less than perfect weather, and by the incredible dedication and knowledge of the experts. At the beginning I was quite nervous about being the non-expert amongst this collective fount of knowledge, but they give of themselves so generously that I can now appreciate a little of their knowledge rubbing off on me. I'm sure the visitors feel exactly the same way.

The smooth unfolding of the day looks quite effortless, but like all well-run operations it would be dead in the water but for the skill and organization of the production team and the crew, many of whom work tirelessly throughout the year to make it a success.

I hope that through the pages of this book you will feel a part of one of the longest surviving and most successful stories in British television history – and gain huge enjoyment in the process!

Michael Aspel

How the programme started

Those who were involved in the first *Antiques Roadshow,* on 17 May 1977 at the Town Hall in Hereford, had no inkling that before long it would become compulsive viewing for millions. Today, far from having run its course, the programme is not only a British institution, but also the largest regular public event put on by the BBC. Over the years the Roadshow has reached every corner of the British Isles and beyond, each event bringing together a world-class team of experts to share their knowledge with a patient public prepared to wait hours to learn more about their treasures. It is a winning formula, and one that is guaranteed to give pleasure to viewers for years to come.

◀ **Angela Rippon and Arthur Negus discuss the day's events with an expert and a customer at the Trowbridge Roadshow, which was filmed for the second series.**

Birth of an idea

Inspiration

To trace the Roadshow's origins we look back to the late 1960s, when the the much-loved *Going For A Song*, the accessible face of antique collecting starring Arthur Negus, was in full swing. This, and another show, *Collectors' World*, generated sackloads of post. Viewers were bursting with questions about their objects. When and where were they made, by whom and what were they worth?

After discussions at BBC Bristol, it was agreed that a programme where members of the public brought along their own objects to show to a team of experts would stand a good chance of success.

BBC Bristol went to observe one of Sotheby's valuation days, where the public could bring along antiques for a free valuation in the hope of generating business. A young David Battie was amongst the experts working that day! The new programme developed along similar lines, but with an important difference: the planning decreed that it would be a public event with no commercial agenda.

Testing the format

Every new programme starts life with a pilot to test its potential. Hereford Town Hall was picked as the ideal venue for the *Antiques Roadshow* trial run. The event was advertised in advance, including the offer to transport large pieces of furniture or paintings that could not comfortably be carried. Filming took place in an upstairs hall – on a much smaller scale than today, but using a very similar format.

At the end of that first gathering the executive producer, the late Robin Drake, called the experts together to discuss the day. What would the powers that be make of the footage, they wondered? They need not have been concerned. One of the great success stories of British television had been set in motion.

▲ **Arthur Negus in conversation with Max Robertson, the show's host, during one of the *Going For A Song* programmes. Max was also the BBC's leading Wimbledon commentator.**

◄ **A young Hugo Morley-Fletcher and Arthur Negus, by then the elder statesman of antiques programmes, discuss an object at one of the early Roadshows.**

◀ A set of four Victorian Street Cries of London silver salts made by the famous London firm of Hunt, Storr and Mortimer. Valued at £20,000 (c.$36,500) in 1997.

▶ A walnut spinet made in 1730. It has its original brass hinges, and ivory and ebony keys with pressed paper patterns at the ends. Valued at £10–20,000 (c.$18,000–36,500) in 1990.

◀ A rare Japanese Kakiemon vase made c.1660–70 and exported to the West not long after Japanese porcelain decorators began to add yellow to their palette of colours. Valued at £9–12,000 (c.$16,500–22,000) in 1995.

▶ A fine porcelain plaque made in Berlin and painted in Vienna in 1880. Young girls with flowing locks are much sought after as subject matter. Valued at £15–20,000 (c.$27,500–36,500) in 1990.

Locations

Series 1: 1977–8

LOCATION	VENUE	RECORDED
Hereford (pilot programme)	Town Hall	17 May 1977
Bedworth	Civic Centre	26 April 1978
Yeovil	Johnson Hall	17 May 1978
Newbury	Newbury Corn Exchange	7 June 1978
Northallerton	Hambleton Civic Hall	5 July 1978
Buxton	Buxton Pavilion	19 July 1978
Perth	Town Hall	28 July 1978
Mold	Theatr Clwyd Complex	23 August 1978

Series 2: 1979

LOCATION	VENUE	RECORDED
Trowbridge	Civic Hall	28 June
Llandridnod Wells	Grand Pavilion	17 July
Ely	The Maltings	2 August
Oldham	Civic Centre	14 August
Maidstone	College of Further and Higher Education	30 August
Camberley	Civic Hall	21 September
Stoke-on-Trent	Kings Hall, Kingsway	11 October
St Peter Port, Guernsey	Beau Séjour Leisure Centre	18 October

Series 3: 1980

LOCATION	VENUE	RECORDED
Salisbury	City Hall	15 May
Monmouth	Monmouth Leisure Centre	29 May
Cheltenham	Town Hall	12 June
Troon	Concert Hall	3 July
Aylesbury	Civic Centre	28 August
Aberystwyth	Great Hall, Arts Centre	25 September
Derby	Great Hall, Assembly Rooms	9 October
Bognor Regis	Bognor Regis Centre	23 October

Series 4: 1981

LOCATION	VENUE	RECORDED
St Austell	Cornwall Coliseum	20 May
Lancaster	Town Hall	4 June
Winchester	Guildhall	17 June
Leamington Spa	Royal Spa Centre	2 July
Bolton	Albert Hall	16 July
Exeter	Great Hall, Exeter University	3 September
Scarborough	Spa Grand Hall	14 October
Malvern	The Winter Gardens	4 November

Series 5: 1982

LOCATION	VENUE	RECORDED
Gloucester	Gloucester Leisure Centre	16 June
Harrogate	Royal Baths Assembly Rooms	8 July
Dundee	The Caird Hall	22 July
Leicester	De Montfort Hall	8 September
Torquay	Town Hall	22 September
Norwich	St Andrew's and Blackfriars' Hall	30 September
Southport	Floral Hall	20 October
Folkestone	Leas Cliff Hall	3 November

Series 6: 1983

LOCATION	VENUE	RECORDED
St Helier, Jersey	Gloucester Hall	28 March
Poole	Poole Arts Centre	9 June
Crewe	Oakley Centre	27 July
Reading	Hexagon	7 September
Aberdeen	Music Hall	21 September
Eastbourne	Winter Garden	5 October
Blackburn	King George's Hall	19 October

Series 7: 1984

LOCATION	VENUE	RECORDED
Plymouth	Guildhall	7 June
Kendal	South Lakeland Leisure Centre	21 June
Banbury	Spiceball Park Leisure Centre	5 July
Nottingham	Sports Centre, University of Nottingham	19 July
Swansea	Brangwyn Hall, Guildhall	6 September
Sunderland	Crowtree Leisure Centre	13 September
Portsmouth	Guildhall	11 October
Douglas, Isle of Man	Villa Marina	25 October

Series 8: 1985

LOCATION	VENUE	RECORDED
Wolverhampton	Civic Hall	6 June
Edinburgh	Meadowbank Sports Centre	27 June
Ipswich	Corn Exchange	11 July
Bedford	Bunyan Centre	25 July
Llandudno Centre	Canolfan Aberconwy	5 September
Doncaster	Exhibition Centre, Doncaster Racecourse	26 September
Hull	City Hall	3 October
Swindon	Oasis Leisure Centre	17 October
Watford	Town Hall	25 October
Southend-on-Sea	Cliffs Pavilion	7 November

Series 9: 1986

LOCATION	VENUE	RECORDED
Barnstaple	North Devon Leisure Centre	15 May
Dunfermline	Glen Pavilion	29 May
Southampton	Guildhall	12 June
Chester	Northgate Arena	26 June
Bath	Leisure Centre, North Parade	3 July
Newcastle upon Tyne	Eldon Square Recreation Centre	17 July
Preston	Guildhall	4 September
Carlisle	Sands Centre	18 September
Worthing	Assembly Hall	2 October
Peterborough	Wirrina Stadium	16 October
Camborne	Carn Brea Leisure Centre	30 October
Margate	Winter Gardens	7 November

Series 10: 1987

LOCATION	VENUE	RECORDED
Worcester	Perdiswell Sports Centre	6 May
Great Yarmouth	Marina Leisure Centre	21 May
Chelmsford	Riverside Leisure Centre	25 June
Cambridge	Corn Exchange	9 July
Glasgow	Scottish Exhibition and Conference Centre	23 July
Cardiff	St David's Hall	3 September
Bradford	Richard Dunn Sports Centre	17 September
Middlesbrough	Rainbow Leisure Centre	1 October
Ventnor, Isle of Wight	Winter Gardens	8 October
Belfast, N Ireland	Ulster Hall	22 October
Maidenhead	Magnet Leisure Centre	29 October
Sheffield	Cutlers' Hall	11 November

Series 11: 1988

LOCATION	VENUE	RECORDED
Liverpool	St George's Hall	28 April
Harrow	Harrow Leisure Centre	12 May
Birmingham	Cocks Moor Leisure Centre	26 May
Bournemouth	Bournemouth International Conference Centre	16 June
Bristol	Brunel Centre	23 June
Dublin, Ireland	Royal Hospital, Kilmainham	7 July
Guildford	Civic Hall	21 July
Leeds	Sports Centre, University of Leeds	8 September
Newark-on-Trent	Kelham Hall	22 September
Hastings	Hastings Sports Centre	5 October
Glenrothes	Fife Sports Centre	20 October
Tavistock	Tavistock Pannier Market	2 November

Series 12: 1989

LOCATION	VENUE	RECORDED
Blackpool	Tower Ballroom	12 April
Manchester	Town Hall	27 April
Lincoln	Lincoln Cathedral	25 May
Helsingor, Denmark	Elsinore Castle	31 May
Malmö, Sweden	Masshallarna	4 June
Elgin	High School	6 July
Leominster	Leominster Leisure Centre	20 July
Northampton	Derngate Centre	7 September
Paignton	Torbay Leisure Centre	14 September

Series 15: 1992

LOCATION	VENUE	RECORDED
Spalding	Castle Sports Complex	7 May
Chesterfield	Queens Park Sports Centre	21 May
Berwick-upon-Tweed	Bonarsteads Leisure Centre	4 June
Aberdeen	Exhibition and Conference Centre, Bridge of Don	2 July
Macclesfield	Macclesfield Leisure Centre	16 July
Kingsbridge	Kingsbridge Sports Centre	30 July
Kingston, Jamaica	Devon House	6 September
Coventry	Warwick University Arts Centre	17 September
London	Kensington Town Hall	8 October
Beaulieu	National Motor Museum	15 October
Pembroke	Pembroke Leisure Centre	29 October
Arundel	Baron's Hall, Arundel Castle	12 November
York (The Next Generation)	National Railway Museum	22 November

Tunbridge Wells	Assembly Hall	28 September
Hornchurch	Hornchurch Sports Centre	5 October
Brighton	Corn Exchange	26 October

Series 13: 1990

LOCATION	VENUE	RECORDED
Darlington	Dolphin Centre	26 April
Merthyr Tydfil	Rhydycar Leisure Centre	3 May
Stowmarket	Mid-Suffolk Leisure Centre	24 May
London	Business Design Centre, Islington	14 June
Hexham	Wentworth Leisure Centre	28 June
Whitehaven	Whitehaven Sports Centre	12 July
Ayr	Dam Park Hall	26 July
Salisbury	Salisbury Cathedral	6 September
St Ives	St Ives Recreation Centre	20 September
Stafford	Stychfields Hall	4 October
Gillingham	St George's Conference Centre	18 October
Valletta, Malta	Mediterranean Conference Centre	3 November

Series 16: 1993

LOCATION	VENUE	RECORDED
Stoke-on-Trent	Grand Hall, Trentham Gardens	13 May
Kidderminster	Forest Glades Leisure Centre	27 May
Cork, Ireland	City Hall	7 June
Beaumaris, Anglesey	Canolfan Beaumaris Leisure Centre	24 June
Exeter	Great Hall, Exeter University	8 July
Barrow-in-Furness	Park Leisure Centre	15 July
Suffolk	Hevingham Hall	29 July
London	Olympia Exhibition Centre	11 September
Crawley	Hawth Theatre	16 September
Ashford	Stour Centre	30 September
County Durham	Raby Castle	14 October
Motherwell	Motherwell Concert Hall	21 October
King's Lynn	Lynnsport and Leisure Park	28 October
Gibraltar	Central Hall	11 November
London (The Next Generation)	Science Museum	28 November

Series 14: 1991

LOCATION	VENUE	RECORDED
Queensferry	Deeside Leisure Centre	2 May
Cleethorpes	Cleethorpes Leisure Centre	16 May
London	Alexandra Palace	30 May
Farnham	Farnham Sports Centre	13 June
Enniskillen, N Ireland	Lakeland Forum	27 June
Chippenham	Olympiad Leisure Centre	11 July
Stratford-upon-Avon	Civic Hall	5 September
Yeovilton	Fleet Air Arm Museum	19 September
York	Barbican	3 October
Hemel Hempstead	Dacorum Pavilion	17 October
Stromness, Orkney	Stromness Academy	27 October
Rochdale	Town Hall	14 November
Bristol (The Next Generation)	Brunel Centre	24 November

Series 17: 1994

LOCATION	VENUE	RECORDED
Colchester	Charter Hall, Leisure World	5 May
Wellington	Wrekin College	19 May
Bridlington	Spa Royal Hotel	2 June
Bexhill-on-Sea	De La Warr Pavilion	14 June
Truro	Truro Cathedral	23 June
Inverness	Inverness Sports Centre	7 July
Bedfordshire	Luton Hoo	21 July
Basingstoke	Anvil	28 July
Derby	Assembly Rooms	8 September
St Peter Port, Guernsey	Beau Séjour Leisure Centre	22 September
Newcastle Emlyn	Newcastle Emlyn Leisure Centre	29 September
Huddersfield	Huddersfield Sports Centre	13 October
Taunton	Blackbrook Pavilion	20 October

Chepstow	Chepstow Leisure and Education Centre	30 May
Cornwall	Lanhydrock	7 June
Penzance/ Isles of Scilly	St John's Hall, Penzance	11 June
Derbyshire	Chatsworth	27 June
Perth	City Halls	10 July
Portree, Skye	Portree Community Centre	13 July
Lyme Regis	Allhallows College	18 July
East Sussex	Micheham Priory	25 July
Horsham	Christ's Hospital, Bluecoat School	5 September
Buckinghamshire	Waddesdon Manor	19 September
London	Indoor School, Lord's Cricket Ground	26 September
The Wirral	Oval Leisure Centre	3 October
Skegness	Embassy Centre	10 October
Pickering	North Ryedale Leisure Centre	24 October
Aberystwyth	Plascrug Leisure Centre	31 October
Saffron Walden	Lord Butler Leisure Centre	7 November
Edinburgh (The Next Generation)	Royal Museum of Scotland	17 November
Arras, France	Hôtel de Ville	15 February
Moreton-in-Marsh	Fire Service College	21 February

Oxfordshire	Blenheim Palace	3 November
London (The Next Generation)	Granada Studios Tour	19 November
Brussels, Belgium	Salle de la Madeleine	21 February
Accrington	Hyndburn Sports Centre	2 March
Wymondham	Wymondham Leisure Centre	9 March

Series 18: 1995

LOCATION	VENUE	RECORDED
Ely	Ely Cathedral	4 May
Dover	Dover Leisure Centre	18 May
Llangollen	Royal International Pavilion	1 June
St Helier, Jersey	Fort Regent Leisure Centre	8 June
Stirling	University of Stirling Sports Centre	22 June
Alnwick	Alnwick Castle	6 July
Henley	Henley Management College	23 July
Cheltenham	Town Hall	27 July
Weymouth	Weymouth Sports Centre	7 September
North Yorkshire	Fountains Abbey	13 September
Peebles	Gytes Leisure Centre	12 October
Penarth	Penarth Leisure Centre	19 October
Windermere	Lakes School	2 November
Mansfield	Mansfield Leisure Centre	9 November
Belfast, N Ireland (The Next Generation)	Ulster Folk and Transport Museum	19 November
Amsterdam, Netherlands	St Olof's Chapel, Golden Tulip Barbizon Palace Hotel	25 February
Broxbourne	Civic Centre	7 March

Series 19: 1996

LOCATION	VENUE	RECORDED
Ludlow	South Shropshire Leisure Centre	25 April
Portsmouth	Historic Dockyard, Boathouse No 7	2 May
Market Harborough	Harborough Leisure Centre	16 May

Series 20: 1997

LOCATION	VENUE	RECORDED
Barnsley	Metrodome Centre	16 April
Fort William	Marco's An Aird Leisure Centre	24 April
Woking	Woking Leisure Centre	8 May
Altrincham	Altrincham Leisure Centre	15 May
Walsall	Town Hall	29 May
Minehead	Minehead Station	11 June
Lincolnshire	Burghley House	19 June
Norfolk	Blickling Hall	25 June
Marlborough	Marlborough College	10 July
St David's	Bishop's Palace	16 July
Oxford	Christ Church College	24 July
West Dean	West Dean College	4 September
Dartmouth	Britannia Royal Naval College	11 September
Durham	Abbey Sports Centre	18 September
Hull	City Hall	2 October
Newport, Isle of Wight	Medina Centre	9 October
Weston-super-Mare	RAF Locking	23 October
Porthmadog	Porthmadog Leisure Centre	30 October
Bolton	Bolton Wanderers Football Stadium	6 November
Cardiff (The Next Generation)	Techniquest	16 November
County Clare, Ireland	Dromoland Castle	27 November
Brecon	Brecon Leisure Centre	5 March
Canterbury	Kingsmead Leisure Centre	12 March
Cannock	Chase Leisure Centre	19 March

Series 21: 1998

LOCATION	VENUE	RECORDED
Bletchley	Bletchley Leisure Centre	23 April
Welshpool	Welshpool Leisure Centre	30 April
Stranraer	Ryan Centre	7 May

Reading	Loddon Valley Leisure Centre	14 October
Clacton-on-Sea	Clacton Leisure Centre	21 October
Keswick	Keswick School	28 October
Machynlleth (Millennium show)	Machynlleth Community Hall	8 October
Eltham (Millennium show)	Eltham Palace	9 November
St Andrews (Millennium show)	Town Hall	9 November
Leyburn (Millennium show)	Methodist Church Hall	9 November
Greyabbey (Millennium show)	Greyabbey Village Hall	9 November

Series 23: 2000

LOCATION	VENUE	RECORDED
Barnstaple	North Devon Leisure Centre	9 March
Biddulph	Biddulph Valley Leisure Centre	16 March
Selby	Abbey Leisure Centre	23 March
Eston, Middlesbrough	Eston Leisure Centre	6 April
Wisbech	Hudson Leisure Centre	13 April
Newport	Newport Centre	11 May
London	Victoria & Albert Museum	18 May
Cliveden	Cliveden House	25 May
Blackpool	Winter Gardens	8 June
Salford	University of Salford	15 June
Glamis by Forfar, Scotland	Glamis Castle	22 June
Chard	Forde Abbey	6 July
Ledbury	Eastnor Castle	13 July
Lochgilphead	Mid Argyll Sports Centre	20 July
Birmingham	University of Birmingham	27 July
Knebworth	Knebworth House	14 September
Caernarfon	Arfon Leisure Centre	28 September
Melksham	Christie Miller Sports Centre	12 October
Rugby	Ken Marriott Leisure Centre	26 October
Egham, Surrey	Royal Holloway College	31 October
Hendon - (The Next Generation)	Royal Air Force Museum	5 November

Series 24: 2001

LOCATION	VENUE	RECORDED
Kettering	Leisure Village	15 March
Hartlepool	Mill House Leisure Centre	5 April
Haywards Heath	Dolphin Leisure Centre	26 April
Newmarket	Newmarket Racecourse	10 May
Shetland	Clickimin Leisure Complex	19 May
Tiverton, Devon	Knightshayes Court	31 May
Carlisle	Sands Leisure Centre	6 June
near Kelso, Scotland	Mellerstain House	9 June
Egham, Surrey	Royal Holloway College	14 June
near King's Lynn, Buxton	Houghton Hall	4 July
Buxton	Pavilion Gardens	12 July
Bridgend	Recreation Centre	19 July
Stroud	Stratford Park Leisure Centre	26 July
Nottingham	Harvey Hadden Sports Centre	13 September
St Austell	Polkyth Leisure Centre	20 September

London	Syon Park	21 May
Tetbury	Westonbirt School	28 May
Suffolk	Ickworth House	4 June
Cheshire	Lyme Park	18 June
Poole	Poole Arts Centre	25 June
Berkshire	Highclere Castle	9 July
Colwyn Bay	Colwyn Bay Leisure Centre	16 July
Ormskirk	Edge Hill University College	23 July
Dorking	Dorking Halls	30 July
London	Greenwich Royal Naval College	3 September
Gainsborough	West Lindsey Leisure Centre	10 September
Plymouth	Guildhall	17 September
Carnoustie	Carnoustie Leisure Centre	1 October
Gateshead	Gateshead International Stadium	8 October
Northallerton	Hambleton Leisure Centre	15 October
Shoreham-by-Sea	Lancing College	29 October
Gaydon (The Next Generation)	Heritage Motor Centre	15 November

Series 22: 1999

LOCATION	VENUE	RECORDED
Lowestoft	Waveney Sports and Leisure	18 March
Oldham	Oldham Sports Centre	25 March
Clydebank	Playdrome	15 April
Morpeth, Northumberland	Morpeth Riverside Leisure Centre	22 April
Grantham	Grantham Meres Leisure Centre	29 April
Douglas, Isle of Man	Villa Marina	13 May
Torquay	Riviera Leisure Centre	20 May
Penshurst	Penshurst Place	27 May
Northampton	Castle Ashby	3 June
Wrexham	N.E.W.I. (North East Wales Institute)	17 June
Athelhampton	Athelhampton House	24 June
near York	Castle Howard	3 July
Llanelli	Llanelli Leisure Centre	15 July
Winchester	Winchester College	22 July
Worcester	Worcester Cathedral	29 July
Coleraine, N Ireland	Coleraine Leisure Centre	16 September
Halifax	North Bridge Leisure Centre	23 September

Ottawa	National Gallery	30 September
Toronto	Casa Loma, exterior	3 October
Basingstoke	Milestones	14 October
(Children's Roadshow)		
Harrogate	International Centre	18 October
Whitchurch	Sport and Leisure Centre	25 October
Witney	Windrush Leisure Centre	8 November

Series 25: 2002

LOCATION	VENUE	RECORDED
Liverpool	St George's Hall	11 April
Tenby, Dyfed	Tenby Leisure Centre	18 April
Tidworth	Tidworth Leisure Centre	25 April
Warwick	Warwick Castle	30 May
Leeds	Town Hall	13 June
Chichester	Chichester Cathedral	20 June
Shugborough	Shugborough Hall	27 June
Renishaw	Renishaw Hall	11 July
Westerham	Chartwell	18 July
London	Mansion House	21 July
London	Mansion House	22 July
(25th Anniversary Celebration)		
Renishaw	Renishaw Hall	11 July
Clitheroe	Roefield Leisure Centre	5 September
Ramsgate	Ramsgate Sports Centre	12 September
Highlands, Scotland	Dunrobin Castle	25 September
Oban	Corran Halls	28 September
Rutland	Uppingham School	17 October
Sherborne	Sherborne School	31 October
Duxford	Imperial War Museum	17 November
(Children's Roadshow)		

Series 26: 2003

LOCATION	VENUE	RECORDED
Bala	Penllyn Leisure Centre	3 April
Abergavenny	Abergavenny Leisure Centre	10 April
Dumfries	Ice Bowl	1 May
Burton upon Trent	Meadowside Leisure Centre	15 May
Redruth	Carn Brea Leisure Centre	22 May
near Bath	Dyrham Park	5 June
Bedfordshire	Woburn Abbey	12 June
Gosport	Royal Hospital Haslar	19 June
Winchcombe	Sudeley Castle	3 July
Braintree	Cressing Temple Barns	10 July
Wisley	RHS Garden	17 July
Kendal	Queen Katherine School	24 July
Co. Down, N Ireland	Mount Stewart House	31 July
Boston	Peter Paine Sports & Leisure Centre	11 September
Scarborough	Spa Grand Hall	25 September
Wigan	Robin Park Sports Centre	9 October
St Ives	St Ivo Leisure Centre	30 October
York	York Railway Museum	16 November
(Children's Roadshow)		

Series 27: 2004

LOCATION	VENUE	RECORDED
Ipswich	Corn Exchange	1 April
Haltwhistle	Leisure Centre	15 April
Hastings	Leisure Centre	22 April

Hornsea	Leisure Centre	29 April
Portmeirion	Village Green	12 May
Surrey	Hampton Court Palace	20 May
Rotherham	Magna Science Centre	3 June
Worcestershire	Witley Court	17 June
near Salisbury, Wiltshire	Wilton House	8 July
Tyntesfield, near Bristol	Tyntesfield Estate	15 July
near Totnes, Devon	Dartington Hall	22 July
Cambridge	King's College Chapel	29 July
Edinburgh	Assembly Rooms	17 September
Manchester	Victoria Swimming Baths	26 September
Cardiff	City Hall	7 October
Stornoway	Leisure Centre	21 October
Edinburgh	Assembly Rooms	7 November
(Children's Roadshow)		
Birmingham	Thinktank	November 14
(Children's Roadshow)		

▲ David Battie explains to Michael Aspel the finer points of distinguishing between ivory, bone and plastic and how to clean ivory. The plastic bottle contains methylated spirits. The "Information Pieces" have proved a popular innovation during the programme and here David pointed out that, while no one should buy new ivory, there was no problem in owning the material that was over fifty years old.

◄ Paul Atterbury expounds on ship model building to an owner.

The team

The team of around 21 experts arrives on site by 9 a.m., ready to answer the questions and solve the puzzles that will be posed over the course of a day during which each of them might look at up to a thousand objects. The full roster of over 80 experts is mixed and matched in rotation from a rich pool of auction-house specialists, dealers, lecturers, museum curators and writers, so that a good balance of specialist subjects and an assured breadth of knowledge can be drawn on at every event. The rapidly shifting field of collecting is reflected in a team that is constantly revised and refreshed, allowing new ideas and young faces to appear alongside those familiar and well-loved characters who have graced our screens for many years.

◄ The team of experts and Reception staff gather for another Roadshow. From left to right, back row: Christopher Wood, Alec Yirrell, Chris Spencer, Tim Wonnacott, Andrew Davis; fourth row: Jonty Hearnden, Clive Stewart-Lockhart, Alastair Dickenson, Deborah Lambert: third row: Simon Bull, Graham Lay, Sophie Dupré, Natalie Harris, Christopher Payne; second row: John Benjamin, Marc Allum, Paul Atterbury, Eric Knowles, Rupert Maas; front row: Lars Tharp, Hilary Kay, Michael Aspel, Henry Sandon and Clive Farahar.

The presenters

The *Antiques Roadshow* has been in the capable hands of only four presenters over its long history. The first series was presented by Bruce Parker and the second and third by Angela Rippon, who then left to join TV-AM in 1981. She handed over to Hugh Scully, who remained the firm anchor until Michael Aspel joined the programme for the 23rd series in 2000.

Early memories

Bruce Parker remembers feeling humbled by the impressively wide-ranging knowledge of the young team of experts who arrived to take their seats during that first groundbreaking series in 1977. They included Hugo Morley-Fletcher, David Battie and Simon Bull. All three remain vital members of the team, their knowledge inevitably complemented these days by a few grey hairs!

A winning start

All new television series start with the making of a pilot programme to test the formula and its potential for success. Few such pilots are transmitted, but the pilot *Antiques Roadshow*, filmed at Hereford Town Hall, was such an instant success that it was included in the first series.

Bruce Parker has fond memories of the experience: "I was walking through Hereford with Arthur Negus the day before the event when a van screeched to a halt beside us. The driver leapt out, opened up the back, hauled out a chair and asked Arthur to value it on the spot. Arthur loved the public so it didn't bother him, but we could never work out how he managed to track us down at that particular moment with the chair conveniently in his vehicle!

"It was a good omen. Our prayers were answered when the doors of the Town Hall opened the next day and the public poured through in great numbers."

The success continues

Angela Rippon remembers her time on the Roadshow with great fondness: "In the early days it gave the public an unprecedented insight into how a programme is made. People are much more blasé

◀ ▲ **Angela Rippon, the presenter of the second and third series during the period 1979–80, sits at an expert's table to admire an object brought in by a visitor.**

◀ **Bruce Parker, the presenter of the first series of the *Antiques Roadshow* when it was broadcast in 1978, still works for the BBC in Southampton.**

about technology and cameras now, but at the beginning of the 1980s it was the best opportunity people had to watch how it was done.

"They stood around the main unit (as they do today) and saw how much time and skill went into recording each item. I think the programme has been a marvellous exercise in public relations for the BBC because people can see something of what they're getting for the licence fee."

For Hugh Scully, the programme was the progression of a love affair with antiques which started when, newly married, he furnished his first house with Victorian pieces bought at auction for £500 (c.$900). He was then invited to present *Collectors' World* on BBC2 before joining the Roadshow. "It is a programme that has maintained its freshness without having to make any drastic changes, purely because of the unpredictable nature of the event," says Hugh. "You never know what you are going to find."

Michael Aspel bears him out: "Having spent many years on programmes where every moment of the recording is planned, it is very exciting to approach a day on the Roadshow with absolutely no idea of what I shall be talking about. The people and their objects make the programme, and we react accordingly. I think the spontaneity of the event is what captivates audiences watching in their living rooms. I feel very privileged to be part of that!"

▲ **A devoted collector shows off part of her vast array of buttons through the ages, in every size and material, to Michael Aspel in the stunning grounds of Tyntesfield House, a National Trust property in north Somerset.**

◀ **Hugh Scully (left), not long after he took over as presenter of the *Antiques Roadshow* for the fourth series in 1981, seen here with Arthur Negus.**

The experts

New recruits

Spare a thought for the novice Roadshow expert! Becoming part of the team of around 80 specialists working in rotation involves jumping through a daunting series of hoops. Even those firmly established favourites remember their very first show, when they brought their impressive range of knowledge with them, but little or no experience of television.

The power of the grapevine

Series editor Simon Shaw is always on the look out for fresh talent. It is often the reliable advertising tool of word of mouth that starts the ball rolling, with established specialists suggesting promising people whom they have either met or heard about.

Once a name has been put forward, a meeting is arranged, and if all goes well the fledgling expert is invited to a Roadshow as an "observer," sitting at the table and dealing with the public but with a constant friendly eye kept on them to see how they deal with the volume and range of objects and how they interact with visitors.

Wide knowledge is key

The depth and range of each expert's knowledge is vital to the success of the day. It is only by drawing on the world authorities in their field that some of the most exciting objects have been identified and filmed over the years. Once an object has been approved and its likely provenance established, the expert may need to carry out some fast research before facing the cameras, which is when a network of superb contacts becomes invaluable.

Working together

At every Roadshow, the resident experts exchange knowledge and theories throughout the course of the day. The mix of specialists is always meticulously chosen. Sitting at the pottery and porcelain tables, for instance, will be four or five individuals whose strengths may vary from oriental porcelain and works of art to twentieth-century studio pottery, nineteenth-century continental porcelain – and, indeed, every general and specialist area in between. Good generalists are also invaluable, as they are the ones who find themselves dealing with the entire range of miscellaneous collectables, ranging from old typewriters, toys and dolls to scientific instruments, plastics and textiles.

Ambassadors for a day

The experts are always aware of the importance of their role in representing the BBC for the day and they are all selected for their ability to work comfortably with the public, in particular making them feel at ease and explaining the history and market value of the pieces clearly. Unlimited stamina also helps. They are often installed at the tables without a break from 9 a.m. until after 7 p.m., but every one of them loves the Roadshow.

The expert team

On the following pages are some of the experts who have worked on the show in the last quarter of a century. Some are are no longer on the programme and the date given is that of their last appearance but they may be familiar from reruns. Others have survived for its entire life.

◀**Silver expert Alastair Dickenson explains to a visitor what to look for and what to avoid when buying a standard Victorian cruet.**

Marc Allum miscellaneous

Marc is a director of Rosebery's auctioneers in south London. With over 15 years' experience in the antiques business, his varied and eclectic knowledge grew from a childhood urge to collect. He deals with works of art and collectors' items, incorporating toys and scientific instruments. As a generalist on the miscellaneous table, his expertise covers a wide area and he has a personal interest in antiquities, South American artefacts and Georgian glassware. As well as lecturing, Marc has collaborated in writing two books and regularly contributes to magazines. He joined the Roadshow in 1998.

Anita Anderson silver

Anita originally trained with one of the top dealers, S J Shrubsole Ltd, and then worked as a senior valuer and cataloguer at Phillips for eight years. She set up her own business 14 years ago, looking after clients' collections, private and corporate, as well as dealing within the London trade. One of her clients is the Salters' Company, whom she is advising on building up a collection of salts, while also working on a book of their collection entitled *Treasures at Salters' Hall*. She also advises on commissioning pieces of contemporary silver, one of which won first prize in the Goldsmith's Craft Council Competition in 1994.

George Archdale miscellaneous

George has worked in the antiques business for over 30 years, training first at Sotheby's and then working for Bonhams before spending five years as an independent dealer in the north of England. He has also been an antiques consultant in the insurance world and spent a year working on *Miller's Antiques Price Guide*. He was a regional representative for Sotheby's for ten years before moving to Vost's Fine Art Auctioneers in Newmarket, then Drewatt Neate in Banbury and is now an associate of Cheffins Auctioneers of Cambridge. George is often found scouring the woods for mushrooms with his Jack Russell terrier.

John Axford pottery and porcelain

John studied Fine Arts at Leeds University before joining Phillips Auctioneers to work as an administrator, which whetted his appetite for the world of antiques and auction houses. He went to the Southampton Institute and completed the two-year course for valuers and auctioneers, gaining the highest marks for valuations and winning the Ivor Turnbull Memorial Prize. John is now head of the Ceramics and Glass Department at the auctioneers Woolley & Wallis in Salisbury, and lectures regularly at the Southampton Institute. He first appeared on the *Antiques Roadshow* in 1998.

► A silver covered dish designed by H G Murphy in 1934. Murphy was the leading English craft silversmith of the Art Deco period, a time when English craftsmen were often overshadowed by their European contemporaries. This is a piece of which Paul is particularly fond.

◄ Paul sits in an oak armchair designed by Robert "Mouseman" Thompson (note the mouse carved in relief on the right leg). He is holding a Poole Pottery plate made in 1935 with a design showing a trawler called *Polly*, which is also the name of Paul's elder daughter. On the table to his left is a Gitanes ashtray, symbolizing Paul's belief in individual freedom, including the right to smoke. On the wall behind is a close-up of a battleship painted c.1944, which is unsigned but is typical of the work of many war artists. Below is a 1930s Heal's bureau bookcase laden with some of his favourite pieces. Top, left to right: three Doulton Lambeth stoneware sculptures; a Dutch Permurende Art Nouveau vase; and an orange polar bear by Minton (1905). Bottom: a 1950s Andy Pandy mug, a memento of Paul's mother, the puppeteer who operated Andy Pandy on BBC children's television; a modern primitive-style ship made by an artist in Cornwall; and a Moorcroft polar bear vase designed by Sally Tuffin in 1987.

Paul Atterbury miscellaneous

The colourful assortment of objects with which Paul has chosen to furnish and decorate his comfortable, unpretentious home is a good clue to the breadth of his interests. Visitors to the Roadshow can always rely on his knowing at least half-a-dozen useful and fascinating facts about almost any object.

Paul began to soak up this knowledge during his childhood. Both his parents were keen collectors, inspiring similar interests in their son. After leaving school he trained as a graphic designer and then took a degree in Art History at the University of East Anglia, before embarking on a succession of careers that enabled him to transform his passions into his livelihood.

While working for a firm of publishers during the mid-1960s, Paul began buying English art pottery. At this time it was still possible to pick up examples of Moorcroft at antiques markets for £5–10 (c.$9–18) apiece. He also began to write and lecture about ceramics, and spent four years as historical adviser to Royal Doulton in Stoke-on-Trent.

Paul was editor of *The Connoisseur* magazine 1980 and 1981, and he has since pursued a career as a writer and lecturer, often appearing on television. In 1994 he was curator of the major Pugin exhibition at the Victoria and Albert Museum, bringing together important pieces by the great Victorian architect and designer Augustus Welby Northmore Pugin, assembled from churches and art collections all over Britain.

If Paul has an interest in something, he makes it his business to become an expert on it; this has led him to write many books, not only on ceramics, but also on railway journeys, northern France and Britain's canals. Other passions include early jazz, war memorials, printed ephemera, sculpture and gardening. Paul has two daughters, Polly and Zoe, and divides his time between London, the south coast and northern France.

David Battie

pottery and porcelain

David claims that his entire career has been a succession of accidents. He has never had the slightest ambition, he says, and even gives a talk entitled "My Unlikely Career." After leaving school David trained as a graphic designer at Kingston School of Art, south-west London, and then worked for three years at Reader's Digest. "I collected old books and decided I'd had enough of the rat race, so I got a job at Sotheby's in 1967 as a book porter. I thought of it as a way of dropping out."

Despite this he's been dropping in ever since, visiting millions of living rooms around the country every Sunday as one of the longest-serving members of the Roadshow (he appeared in the first programme). David moved rapidly from the Book Department to the Ceramics Department at Sotheby's during the early 1970s and married Sarah, their glass expert. They have spent more than 30 years collecting together, their acumen occasionally enabling them to pounce on an overlooked bargain.

David's background in book design may be behind him, but books are still one of his major interests. As well as collecting a wide range of them, he is skilled at bookbinding. "I converted my cellar into a bindery to store all the leather, gold leaf and tools – the fillets, gouges and rolls that you need to use in the process. When I bought the book on geometry (below) I knew that the original cloth binding was incredibly fragile, so I decided to make the hinged box you can see underneath it to contain the whole thing."

After leaving Sotheby's as a director in 1999, David concentrated on writing, broadcasting and lecturing. He is now a consultant to Sworders, auctioneers of Stanstead Mountfitchet, Essex, where he is back doing what he loves most: handling works of art. He is a Fellow of the Royal Society of Arts.

▲ David is holding a Lowestoft teapot of 1770 decorated with flowers. "I've had this piece for 30 years. I bought it in an antique shop for a few pounds. The people who ran the shop didn't know what it was, and in those days neither did I! However, by this time I was working at Sotheby's as a 'baby' cataloguer, so I knew it was early English porcelain, but I didn't recognize the factory." On David's right is a mid-nineteenth-century bookcase, probably by Crace, that was bought several years ago at auction.

The figure painting on a gold-leaf ground harks back to the work of an earlier period, making this a typical Grand Tour piece. The bookcase holds part of David's collection of Victorian books, bought for either their decorative bindings or their illustrations. On top sits Sarah's magnificent ice pail, a Worcester blank, which was painted in 1834 and is highly unusual in being both signed and dated. Next to the ice pail stand a Regency Anglo-Indian ivory deer and a Satsuma vase.

► **David's favourite object is this rare copy of** *The First Six Books of the Elements of Euclid.* **Published in 1847, it was an attempt to teach geometry using colour. "The concept was unutterably silly," says David, "but** it's a magical thing, an heroic failure and I love it. I was knocked down by a motorcycle courier a few years ago and bought the book for $2,000 (c.£1,430) with the compensation. It's a fine example of Victorian colour printing."

Jon Baddeley miscellaneous

Jon is the head of Collectors' Sales at Bonhams, which involves overseeing auctions in Europe and the USA as diverse as memorabilia relating to cinema and Hollywood, soccer, rock 'n' roll, marine, aviation and motor cars. Always looking for new fields of collecting, Jon has recently organized innovative sales such as the Potters Museum of Curiosities on Bodmin Moor; Cornwall marine art at Newport, Rhode Island; and the British Airways Concorde auction in London. Jon is the author of the reference work *Nautical Antiques and Collectables* as well as contributing to several BBC publications on collecting.

Keith Baker miscellaneous

A hoarder of birds' eggs, comics, coins and stamps as a child, Keith is still a collector, although he now looks out for Native American beadwork, watercolours, and jewellery. He began his "antiques" working life by joining Sotheby's European and Oriental Ceramics Department in 1972, before moving to Phillips as the head of Decorative Arts for 23 years. Currently, he is an independent consultant, lecturer and dealer specializing in late nineteenth- and twentieth-century decorative arts. He co-authored *Twentieth Century Furniture* and has been a contributing author to the Roadshow books *How to Spot a Fake* and *A–Z of Twentieth-Century Antiques*.

Rosemary Bandini 2001
pottery and porcelain

Rosemary joined the Insurance Department of Sotheby's after leaving Leicester University with a degree in Modern Languages. She then worked for two years in the Japanese Department and three years in Portrait Miniatures. After her two sons were born she joined her husband at Eskenazi Ltd, dealers in oriental works of art, developing an understanding of cataloguing collections and buying and selling. She is now an independent consultant working in association with the company, and is writing a book on netsuke. She enjoys learning languages and speaks Italian, French and some Japanese. Rosemary joined the Roadshow team in 1997.

Tony Banwell 2002
stamps

Tony grew up in Nottinghamshire and has been a collector of stamps since the age of six. He took a degree in law at the University of Wales in Cardiff, and spent his vacations working in the retail stamp trade. From 1979–80 he was director of Philatelic Services for Montserrat. In 1991, after 12 years at Christie's, Tony joined Sotheby's where he was a Deputy Director, a senior expert in the Stamp Department, as well as an auctioneer. In 2000 he was appointed International Director of David Feldman SA, the Swiss-based auction house.

▶ Harry George Murphy (1887–1939), the Arts and Crafts silversmith, made the silver sugar sifter John holds in his hands. "Paul Atterbury and I have written a book on him and it has been a joyous collaboration because we both feel passionate about Murphy. He was known as an innovative silversmith but not as a jeweller, so I hope the book will help to bring the full repertoire of his work to a wider audience. The sifter was a gift to me from the Murphy family and it means a great deal."

The tall red-and-white vase on top of the bookshelves is of great sentimental value. "It's a Pekin glass vase which my wife Patricia and I bought from Christie's in the 1980s when we first got together. It was made c.1900–1910 and I love red and white together so I never get tired of looking at it."

The painting on the wall behind depicting a master and his pupil was the very first thing John bought for

himself. "My grandfather left me some shares in Tesco, so I sold them in the early 1980s and bought this picture from a shop in Willesden Lane close to where I was living at the time. Financially, it would probably have made more sense to keep the shares, but I don't regret selling them. I'd still much rather have the picture!"

Beside John sits a little porcelain bird given to him by his wife because he loves birds and butterflies, and next to that sits a heavy bronze bowl of huge significance to John. "It's called 'The Greedy Squirrel' and was designed and made by Mosheh Oved, the founder of Cameo Corner where I started my career. He was a great Bloomsbury character who arrived from Poland as a refugee and, it's said, bribed his way through customs with a piece of cheese! He was a retailer, but also made jewellery and bronzes. This came up only recently at Bonhams and I was delighted to be able to buy it."

John Benjamin jewellery

John is a Londoner, born in Tottenham and brought up in Wembley Park. "I was one of those chaps who left school with few qualifications, but I'd always liked museums and art galleries so I felt that I had a future somewhere in that direction."

Not long after John began considering a career, he went with his parents and sister to Cameo Corner, well-known dealers in antique jewellery in Bloomsbury, central London. "My parents were buying a piece of jewellery for my sister, and it struck them that I could do a lot worse than join the company.

"Bloomsbury was still a wonderfully bohemian part of London in those days and Cameo Corner was close to the British Museum. They encouraged me to write a letter asking for a job – and it worked! I started in 1972 on £640 [c.$1,180] a year."

John spent four years at Cameo Corner, qualifying as a gemmologist. "I was like a duck taking to water. Not only did I discover that I had a brain after all, but I loved working with jewels."

In 1976, John left artistic Bloomsbury for the more commercial air of Bond Street when he joined Phillips (now Bonhams), eventually becoming International Director of Jewellery there. He stayed until 1999, when he left to start his own business as an independent consultant and valuer. He's a Fellow of the Gemmological Association and has a DGA (diploma in diamonds).

John vividly remembers his first *Antiques Roadshow* at Alexandra Palace in 1991: "I was there as an observer and committed a complete faux-pas by walking in front of a line-up of experts having their photograph taken. Someone shouted, 'Get out of the way!' and I would quite happily have sunk through the floor! I remember filming a lady's diamond wristwatch, being extremely nervous in front of the cameras, but somehow quite enjoying the experience. I've always felt it was a great privilege to be part of the team."

John is sitting in one of a pair of English walnut armchairs, c.1675. To his left is an English satinwood and partridge-wood bonheur du jour, or lady's writing table, of about 1795, which has little silver handles and shows the influence of Sheraton. To his right is a magnificent Italian marble carving of two lions, c.1820, in the classical style. "It's very much a Grand Tour thing and I love it," says John. "I also like old Sheffield plate, such as this little wine goblet of 1780."

▶ "Isn't this just the prettiest dumb waiter ever made?" says John of this English mahogany example of 1765. "The dumb waiter is essentially a masculine piece of furniture, but this has such delicacy, and is perfectly proportioned. It was an incredible feat of engineering to create the fluted turning on the baluster, especially as all the work was done on a foot-operated lathe."

John Bly furniture

Where better to catch up with the man who claims to live with one foot in the twenty-first century and the other in the eighteenth than in an elegant Georgian living room surrounded by Georgian furniture?

John Bly represents the third generation of a family of antique dealers. His grandfather established the business in Tring, Hertfordshire, in 1891, and the tradition was carried on by John's father. John still keeps a showroom, offices and workshops at Tring, and he took the family business one step further when he opened his London shop, now closed, in 1990. The business is also based in New York.

Although perhaps best known as a furniture expert, John has also gained a great knowledge of silver, ceramics and objects of virtu (a term used to describe collectors' items that show particular artistic virtuosity). He spent several years at Sotheby's at the start of his career, where he worked in various departments before leaving the auction house to concentrate on his family business.

John is also an accomplished jazz drummer, and considered turning professional at one stage. "I have played the drums for more years than I care to remember, but once I realized that I wasn't going to be the best jazz drummer in the world, I decided it should remain a passionate hobby. I'm still playing and still enjoying it, but I know I made the right decision." His son James has inherited his musical talent and is a very good keyboard player. They frequently get together to play into the small hours.

John travels around Britain and overseas on buying trips, but manages to fit frequent lectures into his extremely busy schedule. He is in addition a Fellow of the Royal Society of Arts and a Liveryman of the Worshipful Company of Goldsmiths.

Elaine Binning
miscellaneous

Elaine studied valuation and auctioneering of Fine Art at Southampton Institute. She worked at Sotheby's from 1988, and since 1992 she has been cataloguing and auctioning at Dreweatt Neate in Newbury, where she is a director. A member of the Royal Institution of Chartered Surveyors (on their Fine Art panel), she is also a member of the Regional Furniture Society, the Furniture History Society and the Society of Fine Art Auctioneers.

Adam Bowett 2002
furniture

Adam read history at Oxford and York universities and became interested in furniture while working as a removals man after finishing his degree. He joined Phillips as a porter in the Furniture Department in 1987 and is now a furniture historian and research fellow at Brunel University; he first appeared on the Roadshow in 1997. Apart from writing he finds the time to rebuild his house in Wensleydale and mend and ride motorcycles.

Stephen Clarke 2001
silver

Stephen's career follows in the family tradition – his great-grandfather ran an antique shop and was a freelance valuer. His father still runs his own auction house, Clarke Gammon, in Guildford. Stephen started his career at Christie's South Kensington in 1978, becoming head of the Silver Department at Christie's King Street in 1990 and a director in 1992. He is now an independent fine-art valuer and plays tennis, cricket and golf.

James Collingridge
silver and jewellery

At the age of 14, during the Second World War, James started working at Debenham Storr as an office boy. Over this time he attended evening classes in bookkeeping. He went on to become a sales clerk, largely, he says, because everyone else was away at war, and in 1950, after National Service, returned to the company to work in silver and jewellery. He is now the deputy chairman of Christie's South Kensington, and is a specialist in silver and jewellery.

David Collins 2002
pictures and prints

David joined the Picture Department of the auction division of Knight, Frank and Rutley in 1965 as an office boy. In 1967 he became assistant to the picture valuer at Debenham Coe, taking over as head of department in 1971. The firm became Christie's South Kensington in 1975 and he then became a director; in 1987 he became a member of the executive committee. An independent dealer and consultant since 1988, he appeared on the first series of the *Antiques Roadshow*.

Alastair Dickenson silver

Alastair is an independent dealer in the West End of London specializing in antique silver. His antiques experience started once he was taken on as post boy at Phillips in 1971, later becoming a porter in the Silver Department and then being promoted to cataloguer within months. He has also been a director at both Asprey and Tessiers and lectures widely, particularly on fakes. He plays the guitar, and collects them. He is on the Council of BADA (British Antique Dealers' Association).

Penny Brittain

miscellaneous

Penny had the good fortune to grow up with two wisely appointed godfathers, fervent collectors who fostered in her a love of antiques and fine things.

After leaving school she worked with an architect and interior designer, and then trained as a porcelain restorer. She married and had a family, and when her sons were old enough to go to school she took a one-year Christie's Fine Arts course before setting up the auction rooms for Cheffins Grain & Comins in Cambridge; it is now a major regional saleroom. "I was there to watch the building going up," recalls Penny, "and I built the business up from scratch, doing the valuations, the cataloguing and the selling."

The experience of helping to establish a business proved to be an invaluable one. Before long Penny was asked by the London auctioneers Phillips to set up its East Anglian headquarters. Eight years ago she started another business, this time founding her own company, called the Art and Antiques Service, which specializes in all aspects of buying, selling and valuing antiques.

Now a career move looms as Penny looks towards a new phase in her life. Having a passion for older properties, she plans to combine her love of antiques with their place in the domestic interior, assisting home owners to up- or down-size.

Having recently completed a makeover of a Georgian shop in an idyllic corner of England, she is fully aware of the time and resources required to undertake the restoration of a listed building. She has battled with planners and conservationists while wooing her neighbours who were keen to see only positive change. There is now room for children and grandchildren and an organic garden with resident clucking yellow hens.

▲ On the oak cricket table beside Penny sit two of her most treasured possessions, a Regency penwork writing slope and an Italian porcelain turkey group that was given to her by her mother. "It was her favourite piece," she recalls, "but she gave it to me because she knew I loved it, so I treasure it all the more."

▶ "This bird-bath was the first present my husband ever gave me. I absolutely love it and so do the birds! It's modern, made by a craftsman called Chris Marvel, who lives and works in East Anglia. The material is some kind of resin, I think, but with a marble-like feel and texture. It sits on a chimney pot in the garden and we're forever filling it up with fresh water, because the little bronzed birds attract all sorts of other birds, and they all splash about together."

▶ **This hexagonal gilt-brass French striking table clock, with a mechanism constructed entirely of iron, was probably made before 1500. "It is one of my favourite objects," says Simon. "It's exceptionally early for a portable spring-driven clock, and there are not many like it left."**

◀ Simon is pictured here sitting in a Gainsborough armchair with one of his dogs, Alfie. The vivid yellow silk covering was produced by a French textile company, and is based on silks made in the eighteenth century by the same firm in exactly the same bright colours and patterns. The walls are covered in a cotton made in the United States, printed with oriental scenes and given a satin finish. On the shelves is a collection of archaic Chinese objects, which includes some small jade items and scientific instruments. Their exact purpose is unknown, but they are thought to have been used for mathematical and astrological calculations. "You could pick these up in markets and so forth 25 years ago for very little," says Simon.

Simon Bull clocks and watches

At the time of writing, Simon and his wife had not long completed the daunting task of restoring their house as it would have appeared around 1820, when it had its Regency face-lift. They undertook nearly all of the work themselves. "There was a settlement on the site in 1600, and some bits of that are still here," Simon explains, "but what had once been two cottages were connected and faced up in 1720."

Simon is known as a world authority on clocks and watches, but all things mechanical hold considerable fascination for him. He owns various vintage cars and manages the Formula One racing car that was driven by Jackie Stewart in 1972, and which now competes regularly in a European championship. At the age of 18 he was looking after the racing cars of a patron whose second passion happened to be clocks and watches; it was in this unpremeditated way that he came to develop the expertise for which he is known today.

In 1969 Simon joined Christie's, helping to set up their Clocks, Watches and Scientific Instruments Department. He left in 1976 in order to work as an independent dealer and consultant. Recently he became a consultant to Leroy, a French watchmaking company that has been in business since 1764 and was relaunched not long ago.

Simon is an enthusiastic collector of early timepieces, such as this French table clock (above), probably dating from the late fifteenth century. "Pieces like this were only made for the wealthiest of customers," he says, showing an understandable pride in this object. "In paintings of the period you will often see a small clock or watch sitting on a table. It is really acting as a status symbol. Showing that you had the wealth to possess something like this was the point – its timekeeping ability hardly mattered. After all, no one in the fifteenth century was rushing to catch a train or an aeroplane."

Simon is one of the longest-standing members of the Roadshow team, having been on the programme since the first series.

Dendy Easton
pictures

Dendy has been in the auction world since 1971. He started working at Bonhams as a porter and in 1974 became a dealer. He then joined Sotheby's in 1978 as head of the Picture Department at Summers Place in Sussex, becoming a director in 1985. He now runs the Picture Department at their Olympia salerooms, where he specializes in nineteenth- and twentieth-century paintings.

Josephine Fitzalan Howard
pictures and prints

After reading history of art at Bristol University, Josephine spent a year in Florence studying the same subject before joining the Old Master Paintings Department of Sotheby's, where she gained her auctioneer's licence. In 1990 she moved to the London picture dealers P & D Colnaghi, and she is now an independent fine-art consultant as well as working part time for the international firm of Konrad Bernheimer Ltd. Half Danish, Josephine enjoys collecting eighteenth-century Flora Danica porcelain.

Fergus Gambon
pottery and porcelain

From the age of 12 Fergus has had an interest in ceramics, an interest he maintained throughout his training as a lawyer and a surveyor. In 1994, he joined Phillips Auctioneers (now Bonhams) as a valuer and a cataloguer in the European Ceramics and Glass Department, where he is now a senior specialist and auctioneer. He is a regular contributor to *Antique Collecting* magazine and has appeared on *Going for a Song*.

Geoffrey Godden
pottery and porcelain

Internationally regarded as a leading authority on English ceramics, Geoffrey is the author of the classic *Encyclopedia of British Pottery and Porcelain Marks* (1964). He is the third generation of his family to deal in antiques – his grandfather began the business in Worthing in 1900. On his last day at school, Geoffrey left at lunchtime and began working for his father at 2.15 p.m. the same day. He has an honorary doctorate awarded by Keele University and is a visiting professor at the Southampton Institute; he joined the *Antiques Roadshow* in 1997. Geoffrey was a keen sea fisherman and is now a dedicated bowls player.

▶ Roy is holding the helmet worn by Captain Henry Madox of the 6th Inniskilling Dragoons who took part in the Charge of the Union Brigade at the Battle of Waterloo. The Scots Greys, the Royal Dragoons and the Inniskilling Dragoons charged at 1.30 p.m. on 18 June 1815. "All the senior officers of the Inniskillings were either wounded or killed and Madox brought the Regiment out of action after taking a musket ball through this helmet. The best way to get a feeling of what that battle must have been like is to go to Leeds City Art Gallery where the famous painting *Scotland Forever* by Lady Butler (1850–1933) says it all. Madox had the helmet repaired after Waterloo but over 200 years later the surface is now slightly crazed. If you look at the inside, you can see this wonderfully skilled string stitching holding it together."

Behind Roy sits a very fine helmet of the King's Dragoon Guards, 1871 pattern. "Most helmets are of copper gilt but this one is entirely silver gilt, a rare feature. It bears 17 hallmarks! Even the main links on the chin chain are marked. It would have been made for a very wealthy officer indeed!" Both helmets are from Roy's collection, one of the finest private collections of military headdress in existence.

Roy Butler arms and armour

Roy was born into the antiques trade. His mother and father were in the business and would leave their business card in many fine homes around south London, travelling from place to place in a pony and trap during the 1920s. It was through house clearances in those early days that the seeds of his interests were sown. Badges, medals and numerous articles of military regalia came his way.

When he was eight, Players Cigarettes issued a set of cigarette cards entitled "Military Headdress." Roy remembers "picking up the first card in Epsom High Street from a discarded packet, illustrating a Black Watch bonnet. I still have the set today and, what is more, I now own two of the actual headress used by the artist when he drew them for the series. He spent many a long hour sitting in the Royal United Services Museum in Whitehall."

After service in the army during the Second World War he was undecided on a career, filling in a few years buying and selling. "I was in Kingston upon Thames one day, saw an empty shop and decided there and then to open a collectors' shop. I ran it for eight years, often travelling to Wallis and Wallis (a specialist auctioneer of militaria, medals, arms and armour) in Lewes, East Sussex, to replenish the stock. In 1961 I made the most important decision of my life and bought a partnership in Wallis and Wallis."

By 1968 Roy had full control of the business, and promoted it overseas by exhibiting in various venues across Europe, Canada and the United States. Today, the auction catalogues are sent to subscribers in over 40 countries.

Roy has been with the *Antiques Roadshow* from the very first programme in 1977. He also lectures regularly on the Napoleonic Wars. One of his many claims to fame is that he auctioned the gun that killed Jesse James. It sold for £105,000 (c.$200,000) in 1993.

Roy is a member of many societies, including the Military Historical Society and the Army Historical Research Society, and is a Freeman of the City of London. He lives in a village near Lewes with his wife Jessie, another indispensable member of the *Antiques Roadshow*.

Bunny Campione

miscellaneous

Because Bunny Campione is best known by Roadshow viewers as an expert in the field of antique dolls and teddy bears, it comes as rather a surprise to learn that furniture – and particularly early English furniture – is actually her first love.

Bunny went to university in France and then spent a year working at the innovative Bear Lane Gallery in Oxford, before joining Sotheby's in London in the 1970s. "In those days," she recalls, "dolls and automata were included as part of the furniture sales, so I began learning about them at that time. Women furniture experts quite simply didn't exist then, so, although I was valuing and cataloguing furniture, I gravitated naturally towards the dolls, and in 1981 Sotheby's asked me to start a dedicated Doll Department."

Bunny runs her owns antiques and fine-art consultancy, Campione Fine Art, which started in 1988 – this means she travels widely, finding a broad range of antiques for clients as well as selling and giving valuations. "It is such fun because I handle all types of antiques, including furniture, and of course I never stop learning." She has just been taken on as a consultant to a new Greek museum, and in addition to her own work she is "e-mail secretary" to her husband Iain Grahame, who deals in antiquarian books on natural history and Africana. She is treasurer of the Daws Hall Trust Nature Reserve in Suffolk where she lives. This means there is very little time to pursue her many hobbies, which include skiing, bee-keeping and painting – and she plays a mean game of tennis or bridge. She speaks Italian, French and a little Greek.

Bunny has an impressive collection of 70 soft rabbits, including ten important early Steiffs. Her love of rabbits took root at a very young age. When she was a little girl, only just beginning to walk and talk, her parents gave her a dark-brown rabbit-fur coat with a hood that revealed a pair of rabbit's ears when it was pulled up over her head. From the first day she put the coat on, she would only answer to the name of Bunny, and the name has stuck firmly ever since.

Bunny has now stopped buying rabbits, instead turning her attention to corkscrews, but furniture is still her favourite area. "It's beautiful and practical and, if you buy carefully, a good investment that can be realized whenever you need to."

▲ Although Bunny would love to have a parrot, this is impossible at the moment, since she is constantly travelling around the world. Instead she contents herself with owning this magnificent eighteenth-century cast-iron birdcage – shown to her right – which she keeps in the conservatory at her home. "I bought the cage 14 years ago at the Olympia Antiques Fair," she says. "It's supposed to have come out of a Provençal monastery. The clock once worked and the little feeders swivel round. It's sitting on a low table that I inherited from my mother, which is also eighteenth century and is supposed to have been used as a server for a whole spit-roasted suckling pig. I don't know whether that's strictly true, but it was always known as the 'pig carrier' in my family!"

◄ Bunny bought this charming late-eighteenth-century Italian miniature fitted chest at Olympia 15 years ago. "You might well pay a little more at Olympia," she says, "but where else would you find so many genuine and wonderful antiques under the same roof? I love this little chest and use it. Its surface is decorated in what is known as *arte povera*, or poor man's lacquer, a process by which prints are stuck onto the piece of furniture and are then simply painted and lacquered. The chest is 36cm (14in) by 41cm (16in) and is fitted with graduated drawers."

Bill Harriman arms and armour

Bill attributes his interest in firearms to his grandfather, who owned a cinema and fired blanks from a gun at appropriate moments during silent movies. Bill is now director of firearms for the British Association for Shooting and Conservation, based near Wrexham, north Wales. He is also an independent consultant specializing in firearms and other weapons, a Law Society expert witness, a member of the Academy of Experts, the leading body for expert witnesses and a member of the Forensic Science Society. He trained initially as a chartered surveyor before completing Christie's Fine Art Course.

Jane Hay pottery and porcelain

Jane left her native Glasgow to take a degree in modern history and economics at Manchester University. She then did an MA in African studies at the School of Oriental and African Studies in London and joined Christie's in April 1987. She worked in the Decorative Arts Department until 1995 and in the Ceramics Department until 1998, when she moved to Christie's St James's (joining the Roadshow in the same year). She is currently business manager in the Old Master Picture Department as well as being a director of the company. Jane is a self-confessed crossword addict, plays the double bass and devours detective novels.

Jonty Hearndon miscellaneous

Jonty joined Bonhams, London, in 1979 to become a furniture cataloguer and went on to manage their Lots Road auction rooms. In 1990 he became an independent furniture dealer and he now runs an antiques business in Dorchester-on-Thames, Oxfordshire, specializing in eighteenth- and nineteenth-century furniture and decorative objects. He has been a member of the judging panel for the British Antiques and Collectables Awards (BACA) since its inception and is the consultant editor of the Miller's publication *Late Georgian to Edwardian Furniture*. He is a regular contributor to BBC1's *Cash in the Attic* and BBC2's *Sun, Sea and Bargain Spotting*.

Katherine Higgins miscellaneous

Katherine Higgins is an author, writer and broadcaster specializing in antiques and collectables. Her interest began with a degree in art and architectural history at the University of East Anglia and she started her career as press officer for Christie's. She then moved to Express Newspapers as their antiques correspondent and contributed articles to *The Times*, the *Daily Mail* and the *Daily Telegraph*. She has written several books, including *Are You Rich?* and *Collecting the 1970s*, about the value and collectability of everyday household objects from the 1950s to the 1990s. She is working on a new title for Miller's, *Cool Collectables*, to be published in 2005.

Clive Farahar books and manuscripts

Born in Bedford and brought up in Kent, where he went to Sevenoaks School, Clive was the son of a geologist. But it was books rather than rocks that became his passion when he discovered at an early age that he could buy any number of exciting books at jumble sales with his weekly half crown (approximately 12p) pocket money.

"My notable triumphs included an illustrated book of fairy tales filled with chromolithographed plates, worth several hundred pounds today and, later on in my teens, a copy of Walter Crane's *Flora's Feast* which I bought in the local Oxfam shop for 1/6d (approximately 7p) and sold to a bookseller for £10 (c.$18). That kept me in the manner to which I was keen to become accustomed for some time!"

After leaving school in 1969, Clive accepted a post as a teacher in a London school, but before the start of term a far more tempting opportunity came his way, in the shape of a job at £18 [c.$33] a week with Francis Edwards Ltd, a booksellers in Marylebone High Street.

"And so began my career as a bookseller. I later worked for Colin Franklin just outside Oxford, then branched out on my own with a stand in Guinea Lane Antique Market in Bath, where I met Sophie, my wife. We then became part of a consortium which bought Francis Edwards, but the recession of 1982 hit us rather badly and we put the business up for sale. The company moved to Hay-on-Wye and invited me to be managing director, but we had no wish to move, particularly having bought a house near Bath – and here we remain, Sophie and I, working together as independent dealers. Sophie specializes in autographed manuscripts and letters and I do books and manuscripts."

Ian Harris
silver and jewellery

Ian is a Londoner but spent part of his childhood safely ensconced with his mother and sister in Harrogate during the Second World War. "My father was stationed nearby in the forces and my mother, sister and I lived in a small flat, far away from the bombs dropping on London."

By the age of 16, Ian had decided school had nothing more to offer him and began working for his uncle in the family firm of N Bloom & Son, which he runs to this day. "The original N Bloom was my maternal grandfather. We dealt mainly in silver then, operating from quite a tumbledown eighteenth-century building on the edge of the City. I learnt a huge amount at that stage about silver manufacture and repair which has stood me in great stead over the years, but my uncle was a difficult man to work for and I left to work on my own as a dealer."

There came a point when Ian's uncle realized he needed a West End shop where passing trade would be stronger and which valued clients could reach more easily. A small shop was found, and Ian was re-employed and hatched a plan to stock jewellery for the first time.

"I realized that few women are particularly interested in silver, but that a display of jewellery in the window might draw them in. And I was right! Not only that, but in my uncle's eyes my instinct for business transformed me from the kid he had known into an adult who could be trusted. He spent most of his time buying and I ran the shop from the age of about 21. We've been in the West End ever since at various addresses."

Ian is known for his flamboyant octopus jewellery, and collects other octopus memorabilia including bronzes and netsukes. He is a Freeman of the Goldsmiths' Company and of the City of London and a director of LAPADA. He is married to Natalie, another stalwart of the Roadshow who has worked on Reception for many years. He has three grown-up children, the eldest of whom works with him in the business as an IT expert.

▲ Ian sits on a Biedermeier chaise longue he bought for his first flat many years ago, covered in various antique hangings and cushions collected over the years with Natalie. "I'm holding one of my favourite objects, a magnificent Arts and Crafts silver goblet in the form of an oak tree I bought about 30 years ago. Unfortunately at some point the inscriptions were erased so we don't know who it was made for, but it carries London hallmarks for 1902 and is inscribed on the base with the names of three people involved in its manufacture – the designer, the maker and the person who did the chasing. The base is six sided with mottoes all around it and underneath the words 'Devotion, Unity, Perseverence, Strength, Confidence and Sympathy.'"

Towering over Ian is a painting by an artist called Colin Frooms. "I used to go to a lot of Royal Academy Summer Exhibitions and student shows and often contacted artists afterwards to ask to see other work. I saw this at the end of a long gallery at an exhibition in the Mall in 1973 and was immediately gripped by it.

"At the time I had quite a large Victorian house with enough wall space to take it. It's a whopping 275 x 183cm (9 x 6ft). The artist said he would deliver it and arrived with it on his roof rack! It's a real conversation piece, not just because of the motorbike and the figures in the foreground but because so much is going on in the background including the outline of St Paul's Cathedral and figures playing football at the bottom of Primrose Hill. It says so much about London in the early 70s."

Philip Hook 2002
pictures and prints

Philip grew up visiting art galleries and museums, and drew and painted into adulthood, only giving up when he felt humbled by the masterpieces he came across in his working life. He read history of art at Cambridge before joining Christie's. Philip became an independent dealer in 1987 and was a co-founder of the London-based St James's Art Group. He is now a director of Sotheby's, and also a successful novelist; his latest book is *An Innocent Eye*. An ardent supporter of Chelsea Football Club, he lives in a house that overlooks the ground. Philip appeared on the first series of the *Antiques Roadshow*.

Brand Inglis 2002 silver

Brand was an independent silver dealer in London's West End. He was educated at Westminster School, where he spent free time exploring the treasures at the Victoria and Albert Museum and the interior of Westminster Abbey. He was commissioned into the Seaforth Highlanders and on his return to civilian life joined Spink, the fine art dealers, before going into partnership with the dealer Thomas Lumley. He was a Liveryman of the Worshipful Company of Goldsmiths and a past president of the British Antique Dealers Association. He enjoys searching for late-seventeenth-century and George II rococo furniture for his collection.

Sally Kevill-Davies 2003
pottery and porcelain

Having worked for nine years as a porcelain specialist at Sotheby's, Sally is in the process of recataloguing the English porcelain in the Fitzwilliam Museum, Cambridge. She has also written and lectured on many aspects of ceramics. Married to a vicar, she has three children and since becoming a mother she has researched the history of food and tableware, cooking and childcare. Sally's book *Yesterday's Children* explores the antiques and history of childcare. She bought her first antique, a leather-bound book of poetry, as a small child for three old pence, because she liked its binding rather than its contents.

Eric Knowles miscellaneous

In addition to his appearances on the *Antiques Roadshow*, Eric has contributed to several books on antiques, been a consultant on *Miller's Price Guide* since its inception and written three of their *Antique Checklists*. His recent books include *Victoriana to Art Deco* and *Royal Memorabilia*. Eric has featured as the resident expert on the BBC1 programme *Going For a Song* and on *Going, Going, Gone* on BBC2. For the past 17 years he has been director of Ceramics and Works of Art at Bonhams. He is a leading authority on the nineteenth- and twentieth-century decorative arts, including Tiffany and Lalique.

Hilary Kay miscellaneous

H ilary Kay is an independent consultant, writer and broadcaster on antiques and collectables. She has her grandfather to thank for her long and successful career as a specialist and auctioneer. It was his microscope (above right) that sparked her early interest in things mechanical and scientific.

"I was the only granddaughter amongst several grandsons and was always treated as if I were one of the boys. We had hours of fun examining pond life under the microscope, but I was always fascinated not so much by what I could see through the lenses, but by the way the microscope was constructed. I wanted to know exactly how it worked, how the rack and pinions engaged with one another and how all the accessories functioned. I also loved it as an object, with its gleaming brass, and was impressed by the obvious skill involved in making it."

Although as a teenager Hilary knew that she wanted a career in the antiques business, she did not realize how much opportunity there would be to develop not only her knowledge of mechanical objects, but also her ability to lead a team of people. "I had a place at university, but took a year out after leaving school to work in London. Towards the end of that year I got a job at Sotheby's and, thinking that the opportunity might not arise again, decided to postpone university."

She joined Sotheby's newly formed Collectors' Department in 1977, at a time when objects such as microscopes, typewriters, gramophones, cameras and magic lanterns were beginning to fetch reasonable amounts at auction. Toys, dolls and games were also beginning to be taken seriously by antique dealers and Hilary afforded them the same enthusiasm she did every other category of collectable in those early days. By the age of 20, Hilary was head of the department. David Battie, in charge of Sotheby's branch in Belgravia, was her boss for the first three years. She left Sotheby's in 1999 and, along with Paul Atterbury and David Battie, established the *Antiques Roadshow Lecture and Conference Service*.

Apart from the antiques dearest to her heart, she enjoys pieces of English folk art and treen, ranging from carved biscuit moulds and painted Punch and Judy heads to samplers and naïve paintings.

Victoria Leatham

miscellaneous

Victoria Leatham (*née* Cecil) is the fourth and youngest daughter of the sixth Marquess of Exeter. Her father achieved a national and international reputation as a hurdler between 1924 and 1933, winning a gold medal in the 1928 Olympics in Amsterdam.

On his death in 1981, the title passed to his brother Martin who lived in Canada and then, on his death in 1988, to his son Michael who continues to live abroad. Lady Victoria, who spent her childhood at Burghley House, was appointed to run it by the family following the death of her father.

Victoria sees herself as curator of the Burghley House Collection in Lincolnshire, a splendid treasure house now visited by over 45,000 people a year, and she is currently revising and cataloguing the collection. She also organizes regular exhibitions of its treasures in Great Britain and overseas.

Lady Victoria worked for Sotheby's for many years. She appears regularly on television, not only on the *Antiques Roadshow*, but also as the presenter of the series *Heirs and Graces* for the BBC, which consisted of 15 programmes based on different stately homes around the country.

Lady Victoria is keen on interior design and the decoration of old houses and has revitalized the State Rooms at Burghley. She is much sought after as a speaker on both sides of the Atlantic, as well as running her own antique reproduction and mail-order business, Ancestral Collections. In 1992 she wrote *Burghley – The Life Of A Great House* in which she tells the story of the house and her own connection with it.

In November 1994, De Montfort University in Leicester conferred an honorary Doctorate of Arts on Lady Victoria and, in 1999, Bishop Grosseteste College, Lincoln, conferred on her an Honorary Doctorate of Letters. She is also Deputy Lieutenant of Cambridgeshire and for seven years was Honorary Colonel of 158 (Royal Anglian) Regiment, the Royal Logistics Corps (Volunteers).

She is passionate about dogs and about learning to paint, and is looking forward to her retirement to a proper English village in 2007.

▲ Victoria holds a blue-and-white transitional Chinese coffee pot/wine ewer with metal mounts, bought at auction in the 1980s. Behind her is the stunning painting of Burghley House and its gardens by Jonathan Myles-Lea commissioned by Victoria and Simon Leatham in 1996. Myles-Lea has won an international reputation for his unique depiction of country estates from the air, inspired by the paintings of the Medicis' villas in Italy and Dutch topographical artists of the seventeenth century. He was born in 1969 in the Lake District and went to Malvern College in Worcestershire. He then studied history of art and architecture and the University of London, before spending a year on the restoration of two historic buildings which contributed hugely to his understanding of buildings in relation to the landscape around them. Sir Roy Strong describes his way of presenting plan and elevation in the same image as "absolutely unique."

Deborah Lambert
furniture

Deborah comes from an arts-based background: her father was a literary and arts editor on the *Sunday Times*, and her mother trained as an actress. She became interested in the visual arts during her teens and studied English literature and art history at university. In 1978, after a period as visual arts officer for the London Borough of Camden, she joined the Christie's Fine Arts Course as a tutor. In 1986, she became the director of Christie's Education and she is now international academic director.

Gordon Lang
pottery and porcelain

Gordon Lang is a senior tutor for Sotheby's Works of Art courses and has written books on various aspects of Chinese, Export and Imperial porcelain. He contributes articles to various magazines on these subjects and is a consultant editor for *Miller's Antiques Price Guide*. Gordon is also an Honorary Keeper of the collection at Burghley House in Stamford, Lincolnshire. Reading, from modern American fiction to Italian and Chinese history, and cooking, particularly Italian and French cuisine, are his hobbies.

Graham Lay
miscellaneous

Graham joined the auctioneers King and Chasemore in 1975 as a porter, later becoming head of Sotheby's Auction Valuations Department in Sussex. In 1988 he joined Bonhams, and he was made a director in 1990 and managing director of their Channel Islands auction rooms in Jersey in 1996. After living and working in Jersey for six years, he returned to the mainland and was appointed director of regional operations for the company. In June 2004 he left Bonhams and is now a writer and broadcaster.

Martin Levy furniture

Martin runs the London family antique-dealing business, H Blairman and Sons. He was chairman of the British Antique Dealers Association (BADA) in 1993–4. He specializes in nineteenth-century furniture and works of art, with an emphasis on design. He has written on nineteenth-century furniture for journals including *Apollo*, *Country Life* and *Furniture History*. He contributed to *George Bullock: Cabinet Maker* (1988) and published *Napoleon in Exile* (1998). He is a Fellow of the Society of Arts.

Terence Lockett 2003
pottery and porcelain

Terence's first career was as a history teacher. He then spent 14 years training teachers before helping to set up the degree course in the history of design at Manchester Metropolitan University. Terence is now a collector and past president of the Northern Ceramic Society, lectures to many antique collectors' societies in Britain and overseas and is a Fellow of the Royal Society of Arts. He has written books on Victorian tiles, Rockingham and Davenport.

Frances Lynas 1998
pottery and porcelain

After reading English and history of art at Glasgow University, Frances worked for a London dealer before joining Phillips, where she stayed for five years. She then worked for two years at Sotheby's, with responsibility for British ceramics. She is active in the French Porcelain Society and the English Ceramics Circle, and is a member of the vetting committee for the Olympia Art and Antiques Fair. Currently living in Madrid, she works as an independent consultant.

◄ Rupert holds what looks like a twentieth-century photograph of the surface of the moon, but is in fact a nineteenth-century black-and-white chalk drawing of the moon on paper by the engineer and inventor, James Nasmyth. "I bought it five years ago at Bonhams. It was in one of their book sales, in a folder with a couple of other drawings. I thought it was wonderful but didn't know a thing about it. I just bought it and did the research later. Nasmyth made a telescope and drew what he saw of the moon through the aperture. This is one of the drawings shown at the Great Exhibition of 1851. Queen Victoria was so impressed with them that she invited him to the Palace to show them to Prince Albert."

Behind Rupert is a bronze figure group by the Victorian sculptor Joseph Durham, which Rupert inherited from his father, along with a scene of the coast of Brittany by the Victorian/ Edwardian painter Francis Dicksee. On the wall hangs a painting of *Diana* (*with the half moon in her hair*) by an unknown artist.

Rupert Maas pictures

Rupert was born in 1960 and grew up living near the river in Twickenham with his parents and brother and sister. His father Jeremy ran the Maas Gallery in London's West End. "I went to a local prep school and was a remarkably low achiever. I think winning the 'Throwing The Cricket Ball' contest was the highlight of my time there."

He went on to Sherborne, where he excelled at breaking the rules. "I was nearly thrown out for blowing up the lavatories with a homemade bomb, but managed to survive long enough to pass my A levels and be offered a place at St Andrews University to read English literature. Stupidly, I turned it down because I wanted to go to Oxford, but failed to get in and ended up at Essex University."

He was taught about eighteenth-century country house architecture by Charles Saumarez-Smith, now Director of the Victoria and Albert Museum. "At that time I was a PhD Student at Cambridge, doing some teaching, and he advised me to switch from literature to art history. It was the best thing I could have done."

Armed with his degree, Rupert left university to chop down trees in Sussex. "It was a great life. I worked with a friend. We superglued a log to the roof of our van, called ourselves Bloggs Logs and made loads of money selling firewood locally." As winter approached, Rupert asked his father to lend him money to buy a much-needed tractor. "He wouldn't give me the money, but told me I could work in the gallery for a few weeks to earn it. It was very clever of him! After about four months, I realized what he was up to. I left again briefly to sail a yacht from northern Spain to Boston, but returned to work with him from 1983 and I'm still running the gallery today."

Rupert is married, has three children and remains passionate about books, carpentry and sailing.

Hugo Morley-Fletcher pottery and porcelain

Hugo was brought up on his mother's family's ancestral estate in East Lothian, Scotland, and went to school in Windsor before going on to Stowe. He then went to Cambridge to do a degree in history of art and joined Christie's in 1963.

"I went into the Ceramics Department purely because that's where the vacancy was. It was sheer accident, but after about two months a dealer said to me, 'You're going to be very good at this,' which was rather nice."

Hugo dealt with the entire spectrum of ceramics for some years, but gradually began to specialize in continental porcelain. "Non-British is really my first love and that includes mainly German, Italian and French porcelain from 1430 to 1840." Hugo worked as head of department for 15 years but left his full-time job at Christie's in 1991. He still works for the company as a consultant.

He first appeared on television in February 1965 in *Going For A Song* with Arthur Negus. "I also did several *Arthur Negus Enjoys* programmes before the *Antiques Roadshow* got going – and I've been on the Roadshow team since the very beginning."

One of Hugo's claims to fame is that the state of his fingernails has elicited many letters from viewers over the years. He is a passionate gardener – and sometimes it shows! "I've worked the same garden for 32 years and it's always a challenge and always changing. I enjoy shrubs more than flowering plants. Gardening is a bit like the world of antiques – the more you find out, the more there is to discover."

Italian Renaissance architecture is another of Hugo's interests and he chose it as his special subject when he appeared on *Mastermind* in the early 1970s. People also fascinate him: "The Roadshow is all about the people, isn't it? – and so are antiques. Everything that you see was made by someone, or a group of people, and before the middle of the nineteenth century often to order, so that leads you into the fascinating world of the social history that surrounds all these objects."

◀ Hugo is holding a large lustred earthenware bowl made during the late 1970s by leading British studio potter Alan Caiger-Smith, who is also a friend. "Not only is he the greatest living exponent of lustreware, but he's also a very good ceramic historian. He wrote an excellent book on the tin-glazed tradition. I bought this bowl in 1979, probably just after it was made, from a very good shop in Cambridge called Primavera and paid £65 (c.$120) for it. I should think you'd have to part with about £2,000 (c.$3,500) now for an equivalent piece."

The large painting behind him belonged to his great-grandmother. "I grew up with it and was always fascinated by the perspective. It just goes on and on. I can look at it for hours. My step-grandmother sold it, but it came up again for sale and I was lucky enough to be able to buy it and bring it back into the family. It's by an unknown seventeenth-century Florentine painter."

Neil McRae paintings

Neil is a second-generation fine-art valuer who has his own fine-art consultancy based in Perthshire. He was born and educated in Glasgow and started his career as a saleroom porter with Christie's. In 1984 he joined the Picture Department as a junior cataloguer and soon became an associate director. With over 18 years' experience, he has gained an extensive knowledge of the art market and is a recognized authority on Scottish art. In his spare time, he has a passion for malt whisky, mountaineering and sailing.

Hugo Marsh 2001
toys and collectables

Hugo began collecting Hornby-Dublo trains and other railway artefacts as a teenager and never lost the bug. He worked first for Phillips, specializing in collectors' items, including toys, scientific instruments and photography. Hugo joined Christie's South Kensington as a toy specialist in 1989 and is now an associate director and head of the Toy Department. He has written a number of articles on his subject and was the consultant for *Miller's Antiques Checklist: Toys & Games*. Victorian architecture and the restoration of ancient buildings are his great loves, and he used to collect obscure objects such as telegraph-pole insulators.

Madeleine Marsh 2003
miscellaneous

Madeleine is general editor of the *Miller's Collectables* guides and a respected author and journalist specializing in antiques and collecting. She has reported antiques stories for *The Antique Show* for BBC2, Sky GMTV and *Period Rooms* for Channel 5. She writes a monthly page for *Homes & Antiques* and has contributed to a wide range of magazines and newspapers. She has written many books and has just published *Collecting the 1950s* and *Collecting the 1960s*. Madeleine is a passionate collector herself and is renowned for her love of period fashions, which she often wears.

Elizabeth Merry
books and manuscripts

Elizabeth's love of books began as a child, when she spent long periods confined to bed and read voraciously to pass the time. After gaining her degree, she learned the book trade at Bernard Quaritch, the London firm of antiquarian booksellers, before working for Christie's in Europe and London. For ten years she was an independent consultant before joining Phillips as director of the Book Department in 1990, returning to freelancing in 2002. She has undertaken valuation work for the National Heritage Lottery Fund. Her favourite areas include books on natural history and herbals, and she is also a keen plantswoman and walker.

◀ Behind Geoffrey is a blue chalk portrait of the Countess of Plymouth by Sir Edward Poynter, who was the brother-in-law of Edward Burne-Jones. "I'm passionately interested in paintings," Geoffrey says.

"They're beyond the reach of most of us, but you can still buy nineteenth-century drawings like this for a reasonable price." Geoffrey's border terrier, Rosie, lies close by his side.

▲ **Geoffrey loves nineteenth-century objects, especially Gothic Revival pieces. This pair of open-petalled brass and copper flowers, which he calls "Triffids", was bought at Christie's five years ago. "They're quite big," Geoffrey says, "about 18cm (7in) high with 16.5-cm (6½-in) diameter bowls. When the** light falls into them it bounces out again, creating a wonderful effect." The flowers are the work of **W A S Benson**, a leading Arts and Crafts metalworker who made many props for Pre-Raphaelite paintings, including the crown for Burne-Jones's famous *King Cophetua and the Beggar Maid*.

Geoffrey Munn jewellery

Geoffrey's keen wit and self-effacing manner make him one of the most popular members of the Roadshow team. After leaving school he joined Wartski, the leading firm of West End jewellers, where he worked as a junior. These days he is the company's managing director, but claims that he still sometimes makes the tea and vacuums the carpets!

After a long day spent peering at gems and taking care of customers and collectors, Geoffrey makes a beeline for home. He lives in a comfortable Victorian house with a large garden, which he shares with his wife Caroline and their two young sons. The Munn household also comprises two dogs, a parrot and an impressive collection of 14 bonsai trees.

The bonsais stay outside, well out of the reach of Keiko, the Munns' parrot. "They're not that difficult to maintain, provided that you keep them outside," Geoffrey claims. "Apart from watering them occasionally, I probably only spend two days a year working

on them." He is proud of the fact that every one of the bonsais has been grown from saplings taken from his garden, with the exception of a maple that his wife gave him as a wedding present. He is currently attempting to strike mistletoe, a tricky task that can only be undertaken in early spring. "I got the seeds from Petworth House," he explains, "then I cut into the bark of the apple tree and put them in, and now all I can do is wait patiently."

Every week without fail Geoffrey visits his local auction rooms. "You often have to spend a long time sifting through piles of rubbish," he says, "but you need to stay on your guard, because something can suddenly jump out at you." He has certainly benefited from his perseverance and keen eye. "We bought all the curtains in the house secondhand," he says with some satisfaction. "People get rid of them when they redecorate and you get the most wonderful fabric at a fraction of the cost of having new ones made."

Christopher Payne
furniture

Christopher Payne comes from a long line of furniture specialists. His grandfather, the son of a farrier, was sent to Northampton to train as a furniture salesman and, aged 26, returned to Melton Mowbray, where he started a modest shop selling antique furniture at a time when a Queen Anne tallboy sold for only a few pounds.

He also sold new furniture and made pieces to commission. The business expanded until it filled a Georgian building in Market Place, Melton Mowbray and Christopher's father continued the tradition, joining the company to source furniture old and new to fill the large country houses of Leicestershire.

Christopher was born in 1947 and absorbed the joy of furniture from an early age, spending many hours watching the skilled cabinetmakers employed in the family business.

He read law at university and joined Sotheby's in 1970, initially as a temporary measure, but after just one week he was hooked. London offered a world of experience not available in the family business in Leicestershire. As a porter, he handled a huge range of furniture, pictures and sculpture during a time when the market was expanding rapidly.

By the time he took to the rostrum as a fully-fledged auctioneer in 1976, he was well versed in the requirements of such an exacting, but thrilling, job.

By 1981, Christopher was head of the Nineteenth-Century Furniture Department at Sotheby's, had been made a director of the company and was about to publish his first book, *Nineteenth Century European Furniture*, reissued by the Antique Collectors' Club in 2004.

After 25 invaluable years, Christopher left Sotheby's in 1994 to act as a curator for private collections. He also lectures on furniture of all periods and continues to research and write books on nineteenth-century French furniture.

▲ "I bought this brass model of a locksmith's workshop about a year ago in Paris because I absolutely had to have it. It's just 16.5cm (6½in) high, 38.5cm (15in) wide and 15cm (6in) deep. I've never seen anything like it in my entire career, which makes me think it may well be unique. It was made c.1785 and has been attributed to two French makers, Jacques Constantin and Augustin-Charles Périer, and contains everything needed by a locksmith, including an anvil, metalworker's bench and all the relevant tools. There is a fantastic collection of larger models of cabinetmakers' workshops and other artisans' workplaces in the Conservatoire des Arts et Métiers in Paris. They were made, believe it or not, to teach the children of French nobility in pre-revolutionary France how things were made, so that they understood the skill involved in producing the elaborate objects that filled their châteaux. Louis XVI, who lost his head, loved metalwork, clockwork and all things mechanical and made things in his own workshop. I love the application of metalwork to furniture. I think it's still a relatively undiscovered aspect of furniture-making, where a lot of research needs to be done. You can understand why this model holds such a fascination for me!"

Alan Midleton clocks and watches

Alan became curator of horology at the John Gershom Parkington Memorial Collection of Time Measurement Instruments in Bury St Edmunds in 1986. He remembers at the age of ten discovering a book on clocks that sparked his interest in the subject. He went on to take apart and put back together a clock belonging to his grandfather, but his career in horology did not begin until after short spells in the sugar industry in Argentina and banking in London. He then studied technical horology at Hackney Technical College and is now a Fellow and past chairman of the British Horological Institute and librarian and curator of their collection.

Barbara Morris 2001
miscellaneous

Barbara kept a museum in her bedroom from the age of six. The exhibits included birds' eggs, an eighteenth-century snuff spoon, stones from the Khyber Pass and shards of Roman pottery. After the Slade School of Art she joined the Victoria and Albert Museum, retiring as deputy keeper of ceramics and glass in 1978. In 1979 she set up Sotheby's nineteenth- and twentieth-century Decorative Arts course and became principal of the short courses. She is a committee member of the Decorative Arts Society and first appeared on the Roadshow during the third series.

Peter Nahum 2002
pictures and prints

Peter began his career at Sotheby's in 1966. During his 17 years there he started the Victorian Painting Department and ran the British Painting Department. He was a senior director and adviser on Victorian paintings to the British Rail pension fund. In 1984 he left Sotheby's to open his own gallery in St James's, specializing in paintings, drawings and sculpture from the nineteenth and twentieth centuries. Peter also designs frames, writes and lectures and first appeared on the Roadshow during the third series.

Michael Newman 2001
miscellaneous

Michael was born in Birmingham and moved to the West Country at the age of 11 to go to school. At 19 he became the youngest-ever qualified chartered auctioneer, winning the President's Award in the specialist antiques section. Michael has worked all over Britain and Europe and now runs his own firm of fine-art auctioneers and valuers in Plymouth. He lectures and broadcasts regularly on a range of subjects. An experienced generalist, he particularly loves English silver. He is a keen sailor and lives overlooking the River Yealm.

Ian Pickford
silver

Ian Pickford is among the privileged few who can claim with certainty to have been cradled in the arms of a queen! Born in a maternity hospital by the White Stone Pond on Hampstead Heath, London, he was volunteered to be held by Queen Mary when she made an official visit to the hospital.

Ian grew up in St John's Wood in north London. A quiet and studious boy, he showed an interest in the past from an early age. While his peers conquered the playing fields, Ian wandered the museums and art galleries of London, devouring all the information they held. As time went on, English silver began to hold more fascination for him than any other area of the decorative arts. Peering at hallmarks became his favourite occupation.

Nevertheless, he was destined for university and a degree in physics, until a long conversation with an aunt changed the course of his life. "She told me that I'd have to spend a long time earning a living and wisely advised me to make my passion my career. She warned that if I simply set out to make money, I'd have to spend most of my earnings escaping boredom and frustration," said Ian. "It was the best piece of advice I've ever had," Ian went on, "even if she didn't leave me a penny in her will!"

The world of antique silver is notoriously small and hard to break into. It took several months of hoping and waiting after writing letters to notable firms of top silver dealers before Ian won a place at Shrubsoles in Museum Street, Bloomsbury. He began his six years of training in 1965 on £12 (c.$22) a week.

"It was a fantastic environment in which to absorb knowledge. My job was to catalogue all the purchases as they came in from auction houses and various other sources, and then discuss what we had with buyers. I was dealing with a range of very knowledgeable people, including top collectors and museum curators, so it was a wonderful six years."

In the early 1970s, Ian left Shrubsoles and has been an independent lecturer and writer ever since. He is editor of *Jackson's Silver and Gold Marks*, a Freeman of the Goldsmiths' Company and a Freeman of the City of London.

▲ "I'm holding what I call my Toby jug, except that I know it isn't! It's a small French character jug and was the first thing I ever acquired. I spotted it from my pushchair whilst being wheeled round antique shops by my parents, and apparently bawled my eyes out until they bought it for me. It's very special to me and I've managed to hold onto it all my life!"

Mark Poltimore

pictures

▲ Mark stands before a large family portrait of his grandfather's first wife, the greatest soprano of her time, Adelina Patti. The picture was painted by Winterhalter, court painter to many members of European royalty, but particularly to Queen Victoria. Here, we see Patti in costume for *The Barber of Seville*. "I love the picture and all the stories that surround the couple. My grandfather was Swedish and she was half Italian, half Spanish so it was quite an extraordinary union but a strong one by all accounts. He was her third husband. They lived in a castle in Wales, where she sang to the miners and they to her. She really was the Maria Callas of her day, but she died around 1919 so there are sadly very few recordings of her singing. Verdi, when asked who his three favourite sopranos were, replied, 'Patti, Patti and Patti.'"

Mark was destined to become a paintings specialist. His father and godfather founded the Hazlitt Gallery in London, which became famous in the 1950s. Mark was born in London, but brought up in Suffolk. His father died when Mark was 12, so at the age of 18 it was his godfather who invited him to join the family gallery, where he worked for 18 months before joining Christie's.

"I stayed there for 23 years, eventually becoming chairman of Christie's Europe, having run the Nineteenth-Century Pictures Department for many years."

Deciding on a radical change, Mark then ran the internet business E Auction for two years, spending three days a week in France where the company was based. "We filmed sales and relayed them to buyers' computers in real time so that they could bid from home as the sales were happening."

In 2000, Mark became a consultant to Sotheby's, eventually joining the company full time. He is now chairman of the Nineteenth-Century Pictures Department.

Mark is Lord Poltimore, a title he inherited from his grandfather when he was 21. Poltimore House, the family home just outside Exeter, reached the final in the first series of *Restoration* on BBC television. "It's a complete wreck now, no roof or anything!", says Mark. "It was one of those large houses that became unmanageable and was hit by huge death duties after the First World War. I think it was sold in the 1920s and then gradually fell into ruin."

Mark lives with his wife and three children (two sons and a daughter) in the country, where he indulges his passions for rock music and reading. "I play the drums in a very minor band," he says, "but I'm thinking of giving it up because my daughter is now so much better than me! I shall never stop reading, however. I do a lot of travelling and panic unless I've got at least three good books with me. The history of the Second World War is a particular interest."

Sebastian Pearson 2002
pottery and porcelain

Sebastian worked as a porcelain specialist at Sotheby's before moving to Bonhams, where he became a director. He dealt in Chinese works of art throughout the 1980s, when he again changed direction to run a gallery in Cambridge, concentrating on paintings and works of art. He appeared regularly on the *Antiques Roadshow* from the second series until his death in 2002.

Justin Pressland 2001
toys and collectables

An independent dealer in modern and antique toys, Justin specialized in toys from the 1970s, including James Bond, Corgi, Dinky, Action Man, Scalextric and other items related to popular culture, including music. He regularly appears on television and writes for specialist magazines on modern collectables. He also collects vinyl records, hi-fis and digital watches, and is the proud owner of three classic cars.

Richard Price
clocks and watches

Richard joined Bonhams in London in 1975 and started its Clock Department. As manager and consultant he was responsible for all valuations and sales for 17 years. He now exhibits at major London antiques fairs, notably the three fine-art fairs held annually at Olympia. He travels extensively, finding unusual and interesting clocks throughout Europe. He lectures regularly to police forces, helping them to recover stolen pieces.

Orlando Rock furniture

Orlando joined Christie's after completing a degree in history at Bristol University; he is now a director of the company and regularly lectures for its Education Department. He specializes in English and European furniture, tapestries and ormolu mounted objects of 1550–1840. He is particularly interested in the English country house and architecture of the late seventeenth and eighteenth centuries, and has studied the history of patronage and collecting.

James Rylands 2002
miscellaneous

After studying history of art at Reading University, James joined Sotheby's in 1979, becoming a general valuer before setting up their Sussex sales of Garden Statuary in 1986. A former director and a member of the Royal Institute of Chartered Surveyors, he now acts as a consultant, juggling his time between London, Sussex and Bermuda. A regular presenter on antiques programmes, James is also a charity auctioneer.

Adam Schoon
miscellaneous

Adam Schoon is an independent antiques and fine-art consultant with over 20 years' experience. He also works as a specialist and expert witness for Trading Standards across the UK, and is a senior consultant to Tennants Auctioneers of North Yorkshire. Adam was the consultant to the BBC's *Going for a Song* and has been a judge for the BACA (British Antiques and Collectables Awards) since 2000.

◄ On the table in front of Henry sits the Donald Duck teapot, made by Wade in the 1930s, that he took with him when he was evacuated from London as a boy during the Blitz. Next to it is an Aesthetic teapot made by Royal Worcester in 1886. Among the pieces on the shelves behind Henry is a reproduction Ozzy the Owl drinking cup made for him by a potter in Wales.

▲ One of Henry's great treasures, this plate is part of a unique dinner service made by Royal Worcester in 1926 for Kellogg of breakfast-cereal fame and shipped to him in the United States. The centre of the plate was decorated by Harry Stinton, whom Henry Sandon knew well. Stinton specialized in these Highland scenes, which are based on the paintings of Sir Joseph Farquharson. The service was sold after Kellogg's death and, when the buyer wanted to sell on, Henry arranged for it to be brought back to Britain. The new owner invited Henry and his wife Barbara to choose one of the dinner plates. Barbara made the final choice, and later, on a trip to Scotland, the Sandons were taken to the exact spot on the Finzean estate where Farquharson painted this scene.

Henry Sandon pottery and porcelain

When bombs began to fall on the capital during the Second World War, Henry Sandon, a Londoner born and bred, was evacuated to Buckinghamshire. While other children clutched their teddy bears for comfort, Henry packed his Donald Duck porcelain teapot. His instinct foretold a future as one of our best-loved ceramics experts.

There were, however, other ambitions to fulfil. Henry trained at London's Guildhall School and had a successful career as a singer and as a music teacher at Worcester Grammar School and a lay clerk in the cathedral choir.

Archaeology was another of Henry's passions and, while he was excavating his garden in Worcester, he uncovered several Roman pots. "It was the most exciting thing, to find those pieces in my garden. I began to study and research ceramics of all kinds, which led me to the Royal Worcester factory." Henry acquired such expertise that in 1966 he became Curator of the Dyson Perrins Museum at the factory, a position he held until 1982. He joined the Roadshow, meanwhile, during the second series.

"The age of a piece doesn't worry me, or its condition, but it must speak to me, tell me it wants to be found," says Henry. "Working at Royal Worcester, I met many of the artists and craftsmen, and now when I look at an object I'm able to say, 'I remember him painting that plate or modelling that vase or figure.' It gives me a tremendous thrill because it brings pieces alive if you imagine who made them and the people who used them."

Henry's undying enthusiasm for pots still has him scouring shops and markets, and even beachcombing – every shelf and corner of his house is filled with his treasures. He is committed to keeping up the tradition of handmade ceramics, and is a director of the Brontë Company in Malvern which has produced both a Henry Sandon candle extinguisher and a character jug. He has appeared on *Desert Island Discs* and *This Is Your Life*.

John Sandon

pottery and porcelain

John is a Worcester lad through and through, born with clay in his blood. He went to school next to the Cathedral and not far from the Worcester porcelain works, and was scrambling about in the garden excavating pots with his father Henry by the time he was five years old.

"I had a feel for pottery and porcelain almost before I could walk. During the 1960s, when the heart of old Worcester was being demolished in the name of progress, my father and I went onto the building sites to rescue pots.

"We found complete Bellarmine jugs, Roman pots, slipware, and entire sets of delft tiles around old fireplaces. When Dad then became curator of the museum at the Worcester factory, he began the first of many excavations of the original factory, demolished in the 1950s.

"From the age of nine, I was sorting and analysing blue-and-white Worcester patterns, sneaking out of school whenever I could to visit the site. By 14, I was taking groups of tourists around the Royal Worcester factory and museum. I also spent time watching famous decorators and modellers like Harry Davis and Doris Lindner at work. They were incredibly good to me and let me have a go. It gave me a great understanding. I got the history from my father and the manufacturing side from the people working in the factory."

At the age of 16, in the mid-1970s, John threw up his A levels to join Phillips Auctioneers (now part of Bonhams) and is now head of the Glass and Ceramics Department. "It was a great shock for a little Worcester lad to arrive in London and be pitched into the international auction world. What a place to learn! The collectors, dealers and other experts couldn't have been more helpful."

John lived with family friends near Portobello Road and spent glorious Saturdays picking up bargains. "I bought around 150 pieces of early blue-and-white Worcester and Caughley there because dealers didn't know as much as they do now. When I got married in 1982, I sold it all to help buy our first house, but once we'd settled, I started again. Ancient glass is one of my great interests. There is something magical about the iridescence created by things being buried in the ground."

▲ Beside John, on a nineteenth-century Worcester potter's wheel, sits one of his great finds, a Meissen candelabrum of 1740–5, possibly by Kändler, the most famous modeller at Meissen of the period. "Much as I love the charm of English eighteenth-century porcelain, you can't beat Meissen for sheer quality. I spotted this on my honeymoon in the United States in a little gift shop in the Illinois town of Long Grove. It had plastic candles stuck in the nozzles covered with frilly lampshades and had been converted to electricity.

I think the shop owner thought it was a 1930s lamp, but the rococo shape sang to me across the shop. The closer I got, the better it looked! I bought it for $100 [c.£55]. It's a rare model and probably worth around £5,000 [c.$9,000]." Behind John sits some of his wide and eclectic range of pottery and porcelain, including Meissen figures which are loved equally by his wife Christine. "I have everything on open shelves because I like to be able to pick things up easily and hold them. Of course, my poor children (Elizabeth, 18, and Robert, 14) aren't allowed to have parties!"

Chris Spencer pottery and porcelain

Chris nursed ambitions to be an actor but became a teacher instead. He left teaching ten years ago and developed his interest in antiques into a full-time business. He runs a valuations company, owns an antique shop in Falmouth, Cornwall and acts as a consultant editor to various annual antiques guides. He has also acted as a judge for the British Antiques and Collectables Awards. His main interest is English ceramics and other interests include English paintings, garden design and Arts and Crafts architecture. Together with his wife, Suzan, he is currently restoring a large Georgian garden.

Philip Taubenheim miscellaneous

Philip's parents ran an antiquarian bookshop in the Oxfordshire town of Burford, so he gained much early experience of salerooms. On leaving school he worked for a firm of auctioneers in Cirencester, and in 1982 joined the Fine Art Department of auctioneers Sandoes, in Wotton-under-Edge, Gloucestershire. With colleagues, he bought the company that has now expanded to become the largest in the Cotswolds and trades as Wotton Auction Rooms. He is still interested in books and also collects treen, but currently devotes every moment to running his business.

Paul Viney miscellaneous

Paul began his career at the Ashmolean Museum in Oxford, followed by a course in fine arts at the Victoria and Albert Museum. He then worked for the National Trust at Waddesdon Manor, the former Rothschild house near Aylesbury, Buckinghamshire, before joining Phillips, where he was vice president in New York for three years and European director from 1986 to 1992. Paul is now managing director of Woolley & Wallis, the Salisbury auctioneers. He is well known to Radio 2 listeners for his annual Children in Need auctions with Terry Wogan, frequently lectures on the fine-art world and conducts a popular antiques quiz.

Peter Waldron 2001
silver

Peter was a senior director of Sotheby's, responsible for the Silver, Objects of Vertu and Portrait Miniatures Departments until his retirement at the end of 2002. He now divides his time between travelling and research and evaluation of the subjects that have been a central part of his life for 40 years. He appeared on the *Antiques Roadshow* from the second series. Peter is a Liveryman of the Worshipful Company of Goldsmiths and a Freeman of the City of London. He is an internationally recognized expert in the field of English silver, and is also well respected for his researches in heraldry and family histories.

◀ Stephen holds his favourite instrument, a viola da gamba by the best living maker of these instruments, Dietrich Kessler, who is now retired. "This one was made in the 1960s to an earlier design. There are very, very few original instruments because most of them have been adapted to suit modern playing and really, one has to buy a modern example in order to create a sound that is compatible with the people one is playing with."

On the chest beside Stephen is a favourite drawing, a self portrait by Charles Samuel Keene, best known as an illustrator of *Punch* and a caricaturist. "What isn't so appreciated is that he was also a superb draughtsman and highly admired by Degas," says Stephen. "I found this wonderful little drawing a few years ago. It was unattributed because most images of Keene show him with a moustache. I was able to identify it because of the outline of a fez, another typical characteristic of his, and because of the technique he used. There's a lot of cross-hatching around the eyes which betrays his initial training as a printmaker. I can honestly say it's one of the most compelling images I own."

Stephen Somerville pictures

After many formative years living in Blackheath after the Second World War, Stephen moved to be near other members of the family in Suffolk.

"By that time I had become very involved in early music and played frequently with Dolmetsch, the performer and instrument maker who revived and saved the interest in early music in this country. I did think for a time that I would make it my career, but a family member had an art gallery at Aldeburgh and I was given the opportunity to run it as a commercial enterprise from the age of 18."

Stephen's early adult life was a time of intense activity. "I ran the gallery, put on contemporary exhibitions and did all my own mounting and framing as well as playing the viola da gamba and recorder, dancing and playing a huge amount of tennis."

A chance telephone conversation with a colleague led to Stephen joining Sotheby's, and at the tender age of 22, in 1965, he became the head of the Print Department in New York. "I then returned to London and went to work for P & D Colnaghi in 1967, where I was the youngest director and looked after the English watercolours and drawings."

In 1975 Stephen left to set up a business with a colleague, but struck out entirely on his own in 1986 and now spends his working life advising collectors on the assembling and dispersal of paintings.

His passion for dancing, tennis and music continues unabated. Stephen has been married since 1965 and has three grown-up sons. To his great delight, twin granddaughters were born recently. "They're a wonderful addition to the family!" he concludes.

▶ "I'm holding a Clarice Cliff teapot from a 'Tea for Two' set which I bought from a friend when I was 19 in 1974 for £18 [c.$33]. He was a fellow enthusiast and, like me, is still in the antiques business today.

"Behind me is a portrait of Betty Joel, the well-known British designer of Art Deco furniture, rugs and textiles who was my great aunt. She had an influence on me, but I didn't actually meet her until I was in my teens. She gave me one or two bits of furniture including a little stepped bookcase of which I'm very fond.

"Next to me is a Chinese famille-rose export vase of c.1760, made for the south-east Asian rather than the European market. I treasure it because it was given to me by a lady I remember so well. I went to see her whilst working for Sotheby's. Her house had been bombed during the

war and she'd simply scooped everything into tea chests. We salvaged everything worth selling and she then invited me to pick up any broken bits I thought I could piece together. I found all the bits for this vase and had it restored.

"The slender, pear-shaped blue-and-white Wanli vase behind me is from the same source and was in 20 or 30 pieces. It stands next to a nineteenth-century copy of a Kangxi piece given to me by Betty Joel, whose father had been in China and bought it thinking it was older than it is.

"Sitting next to to the vases is a metal gorgette, a curious little neck ornament worn by officers in the eighteenth and nineteenth centuries. It hung just belong the throat, looking like a shrunken breastplate. It bears the crest for the 53rd Regiment, a regiment of foot in the Peninsular War."

Clive Stewart-Lockhart miscellaneous

C live cannot remember a time when the idea of objects did not fascinate him. "I sent off for a Sotheby's catalogue of Post-Impressionist paintings in 1970 whilst I was still at school.

"I must have seen it publicized somewhere and knew I just had to have it. I seem to remember it was a single-owner collection belonging to a well-known American and I sent off a cheque or postal order for 25 shillings, the equivalent today of £1.25 [$2]!"

The catalogue provided hours of pleasure. "I pored over it for days. It definitely set my career in motion. I realized, even then, that I'd probably never have the sort of money to buy all the things I loved, but by being an auctioneer I could do the next best thing; handle them and learn about them. It never occurred to me to become an antiques dealer. That requires far too much nerve!"

The world of the top auction houses is small and notoriously competitive, but the doors opened for Clive, who spent periods early in his career at both Sotheby's and Bonhams. It was during his second spell at Sotheby's that he met and married his wife Jane, in 1982. They have three sons, two of them grown up.

With a family to consider, life outside London began to have enormous appeal and Clive joined the Newbury auctioneers Dreweatt Neate in 1982. He remains there to this day, specializing in oriental porcelain and works of art, books and paintings.

Considering his passions, it seems quite appropriate that we see Clive surrounded by some of his favourite objects against a backdrop of glorious Nina Campbell wallpaper featuring oriental vases, found by Jane when they moved into their house ten years ago.

Harry Williams-Bulkeley silver

After a short spell as a part-time assistant in the National Trust, Harry joined Christie's in Rome as an assistant porter for a short time, before studying history of art at Manchester University. He rejoined Christie's in 1990 and has been with the company ever since, becoming head of their King Street Silver Department in 1995 and a director in 2000. He was closely involved with the sales of the Rothschild and Wernher Collections and more recently with the sale of over 18,000 pieces of silver from the Royal Prussian Collection.

Dominic Winter books

Dominic has been in the auction business since 1972. After a brief shop-floor apprenticeship with a local firm in Kingston-upon-Thames, Surrey, he moved to Bristol for the opportunity to wield the auctioneer's hammer. He spent nearly 15 years in Bristol and created a thriving book department where previously there was none. Since 1987 he has been running his own auction rooms in Swindon, Wiltshire, specializing in the sale and valuation of old and rare printed books, historical documents and autographs.

Christopher Wood
pictures and prints

A specialist in Victorian art, Christopher is the author of *The Dictionary of Victorian Painters*, the standard work of reference on the subject, in addition to many other books on painting. He joined Christie's in 1963, becoming director of its Nineteenth-Century Paintings Department. Since 1977 he has run his own business in London's West End and currently works privately, specializing in Pre-Raphaelite and Victorian art and Gothic Revival and Arts and Crafts furniture. He has a Gothic Revival house that reflects his passion for the architecture of the period. His other interests include gardening and jazz.

Henry Wyndham 1994
pictures and prints

Before his appointment as chairman of Sotheby's in 1994, Henry was an independent dealer, picture consultant and member of the London-based St James's Art Group. He was also formerly head of department at Christie's in London and in New York. His interests range from Old Masters to British paintings, modern and contemporary art and studio pottery. He is a Liveryman of the Goldsmiths' Livery Company, a Trustee of the Prince of Wales Drawing School, a Trustee of Glyndebourne Opera, a former committee member of the MCC and chairman of the Arts and Library Committee of the MCC.

Lars Tharp
pottery and porcelain

Lars was born in Copenhagen and left Denmark for England at the age of six. His archaeologist grandfather was a Bronze Age expert and Keeper of Antiquities at the National Museum, Copenhagen. Through him Lars first became interested in "old things", eventually going on to read Archaeology at Caius College, Cambridge. Being a keen amateur 'cellist Lars spent as much time playing in university orchestras as on his official studies. Graduating in 1976 Lars soon discovered that job prospects for Palaeolithic archaeologists were limited. "The world wasn't holding its breath" says Lars. "However, owing to my own college having Joseph Needham – the 20th century's foremost Western expert on Chinese culture – as Master, I had become drawn to things Chinese."

To pursue this growing interest Lars decided to work for one of the major London auction houses. "I joined Sothebys first as a junior cataloguer, later becoming a director and auctioneer of the firm. Later – in 1985 – my then boss, David Battie, made the mistake of suggesting me for The Antiques Roadshow: we've been competing for the cameras ever since". Lars left full-time auctioneering in 1993 in order to set up his own ceramics and art consultancy, advising individuals, private and public institutions including museums. Today he combines his work with a busy schedule of broadcasting, writing and lecturing. He travels widely, is a frequent visitor to China and is in much demand as a speaker covering a diverse range of subjects: from ceramic history to a passion for the works, life and times of William Hogarth.

Lars and his wife Gillian have two daughters, and live in the heart of the country, along with Basil [shown], their faithful black Labrador. He is a Fellow of the Royal Society of Arts, a Liveryman of the Worshipful Company of Weavers and a Freeman of the City of London.

▲ The work of William Hogarth is one of Lars's abiding passions – his book *Hogarth's China* describes the ceramics depicted in Hogarth's paintings and vice versa. The engraving on the wall behind him is the second in a series of six taken from Hogarth's *The Harlot's Progress*. In this scene, Moll Hackabout trips over a tea table, sending the precious Chinese porcelain crashing to the floor. On Lars's mantelpiece is a Staffordshire equestrian figure of c.1860; it was a farewell gift from the staff at Sotheby's Ceramics Department, who took the headless figure, attached a photograph of Lars and inscribed it on the base: "A Pride Goeth Before the Fall." To the left of the Staffordshire figure are a black-glazed jug and beer mug, a late-seventeenth-century Chinese vase and a magnificent English delftware plate, c.1760, which was probably made in Bristol.

▶ **While filming the American version of *The Great Antiques Hunt*, Lars found this wonderful Chinese famille rose porcelain wall vase, c.1820, in the form of a hand clutching a peach. The owner** wanted $35 (c.£25) but knocked it down to $25 (c.£18) because she liked Lars's English accent. "It's about 15cm (6in) long, worth £2–300 [c.$350–550], and I hang it on the wall and keep my pens in it," he says.

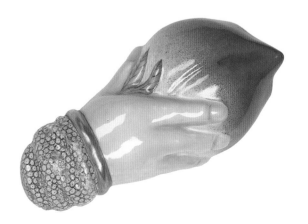

◀ Tim has become absorbed by the life and designs of Christopher Dresser over the last five years and made a collection of pieces, one of which he holds. "This is an iconic Dresser design, either a toast rack or a letter rack. I bought it a year ago at an antiques fair for only £120 [c.$200]. It's got the lozenge mark on the base and the makers' mark of Hukin & Heath, so it was a remarkable bargain. It's worth around £1,000 [c.$1,800]. Dresser worked in the nineteenth century but was way ahead of his time. He was the godfather of twentieth-century design. He embraced the concept of good design being available and affordable through mass production, which I think was a laudable attitude. I was absolutely thrilled that the Victoria and Albert decided to stage a major Dresser exhibition recently." Behind Tim is one of a group of four paintings of African birds he owns, done in the 1870s by Henry Stacey Marks, once part of the Canadian estate of Lord Beaverbrook.

Tim Wonnacott miscellaneous

Tim's family ran a small family auctioneering business in north Devon. "We sold houses, land, animals and chattels. Growing up, I became very drawn to the chattel sales and qualified as a chartered surveyor and auctioneer, but as I got more and more interested in furniture and objects, my father advised me to trot off to London and try my luck with the major auction houses."

Tim took a course at the Study Centre for the Fine and Decorative Arts run by the Victoria and Albert Museum and then struggled to break into the international saleroom world. "It was hard to find a job, but I got one eventually in the Valuation Department at Phillips where I learnt a tremendous amount over two years under the chairman at the time, Christopher Weston."

A period in California led to a job at Sotheby's in New York and a long period with the firm in Belgravia, Bond Street, Chester and Billingshurst in Sussex, peppered with regular trips on Sotheby's behalf to far-flung and exotic locations. "I went to India every year for ten years and was delighted when I was able to take the first three-day sale there."

After over 20 years with Sotheby's, latterly as chairman of Sotheby's Billingshurst and Sotheby's Olympia, Tim decided to focus on his television career and is now the daytime presenter of *Bargain Hunt* as well as appearing regularly on the *Antiques Roadshow*. He also finds time to run an antiques consultation business and his own television production company, Wonna Productions Ltd. Tim is married and has three children.

Unsung heroes

Experts on Reception

A number of experts fulfil the vital and demanding role of receiving customers at Reception and directing them to the right area. Important objects are often identified at this stage.

Sonia Archdale reception

Sonia has had a lifelong fascination with antiques, in particular with adapting the old into fashionable fitments to decorate the home. A year in South America sparked her interest in native antiquities which she now collects. Sonia's other special interests lie in domestic and childhood memorabilia and early-twentieth-century art. Sonia is married to George Archdale who has been a specialist on the *Antiques Roadshow* for many years.

Margie Cooper
furniture round and reception

Margie is an antique dealer and consultant living and working in Prestbury, Cheshire. So absorbing is this career that she finds little time to spare for outside interests. She started her working life as a fashion model and began buying furniture and objets d'art for her home as a hobby. Her interest in antiques developed into such a passion that she opened her own business in 1978. Her particular love is English furniture, but she now deals mainly in silver and Victorian jewellery. She has been a judge on the panel of the British Antiques and Collectables Awards since 2000.

Andrew Davis
furniture round and reception

Andrew trained as a lawyer and then worked as a teacher
and an advertising copywriter before beginning to buy and
sell clocks as a sideline. His interest in preserving objects
grew until he started a career in antiques, repairing and
selling clocks around the country. He went on to run a stall
in London's Portobello Road market for two years and is
now a general dealer in Kew, West London. His main
interests are clocks, nineteenth-century ceramics and
artefacts of 1700–1900, especially country furniture.
He is a member of the Regional Furniture Society.

Sophie Dupré reception

Sophie, Clive Farahar's wife, started her career in publishing.
After being asked to organize the sale of a large collection
of nineteenth-century literary letters, she emerged into the
world of antiques with autograph letters, manuscripts,
signed photos and literary property as a strong interest.
She then ran the Autograph Department of Francis
Edwards Ltd in London. In 1983 she left to bring up her
family, and she continues to run a successful international
business selling autograph letters and manuscripts to
institutions and private collectors. She is one of the
world's leading experts in royal manuscript material.

Natalie Harris reception

Natalie, who is married to Ian Harris, has been dealing
in fine jewellery for 20 years, both independently and in
association with N Bloom & Sons. She studied enamelling
and silversmithing at London's Sir John Cass
Goldsmiths' College and went on to learn the art of
enamel restoration, specializing in Art Nouveau
translucent and plique à jour enamelling. She is also a
Fellow of the Gemmological Association and collects
nineteenth-century textiles, especially beadwork. She has
a fine collection of Indian beadwork and glass obelisks.

Rosamund Hinds-Howell reception

Rosamund has spent all of her working life in the art world,
both in galleries and in public relations. She studied at
Kingston Art School before joining Sotheby's, accumulating
her knowledge of antiques while running the Valuations
Counter, where she dealt with ceramics and glass as well
as oriental objects and works of art. She also worked as
senior press officer at Sotheby's, leaving in 1984. She spent
six years at the Christopher Wood gallery and now works on
a part-time basis for William Drummond, a long-established
leading dealer in watercolours. Rosamund lives in London
and is passionate about opera and gardening.

Nicholas Mitchell
furniture round and reception

Nicholas has spent all his working life in the antiques trade. For over 20 years he has been involved in almost every facet of antiques, from owning a shop to working as an auctioneer and from restoring pieces to giving lectures to others on the subject. His areas of greatest knowledge and expertise include clocks – on which he has written articles for the specialist magazine *Antique Collector* – and nineteenth-century furniture. Nicholas lives near the River Thames in London and canoes on the river. He is also a keen cyclist and holds a pilot's licence.

Fiona Malcolm writer

Fiona Malcolm is a highly experienced antiques journalist. She is currently Antiques Correspondent for the best-selling *BBC Homes & Antiques* magazine and has been associated with the *Antiques Roadshow* since 1988 as a journalist and writer. She attends almost every Roadshow keeping a watching brief over both the recordings and the more interesting objects that do not make it to the screen. She has contributed most of the text to both the *21 Years of The Antiques Roadshow* and this book. Her own special interest in the field of collecting is porcelain. She lives in Kent with her husband and two children.

Barley Roscoe reception

After university at Bristol, Barley studied woven and printed textiles at the Surrey Institute of Art and Design in Farnham, and then established the craft collection and archive at the Holbourne Museum and Crafts Study Centre in Bath, where she subsequently became director. Following a recent move to Cambridge, she has been working as a consultant curator, writer and lecturer concentrating mainly on twentieth-century British crafts. She is also an Associate of the Museums Association and a Fellow of the Royal Society of Arts, and was awarded the MBE in 1993 in recognition of her work at the Holbourne Museum.

Deborah Scott reception

Deborah Scott started her career in antiques when she worked in a flourishing business dealing in antique porcelain and pottery. Having bought at auction, washed up and sold everything from Chelsea, and even Vezzi, to Mason's Ironstone, she then moved on to work for a leading magazine on antiques, the *Antique Collector*. There she researched and wrote articles on many different kinds of antiques – from rocking horses and antique oriental rugs to porcelain scent bottles, fans and fountain pens. She continues to work as a freelance writer and editor. Her particular interests include English porcelain, glass and textiles.

John Bone designer

John started his television career 40 years ago assisting on the first series of *Going for a Song* with Arthur Negus and has been on the Roadshow production team for the past 14 years. He studied interior and furniture design at art college and worked in contract furnishing design and later as an interior designer for a well-known pub and restaurant chain. John's BBC career includes designing several award-winning children's programmes, major location dramas and drama documentaries including Jane Austen's *Mansfield Park*, Tom Sharpe's *Blott on the Landscape* and Gerald Durrell's *My Family and other Animals*.

Michele Burgess producer

Michele's first job at the BBC was as a secretary on *Woman's Hour*. Later, at BBC Manchester, she worked on a range of entertainment, factual and children's programmes alongside the likes of David Essex, Alan Whicker, Russell Harty and John Noakes and Shep. In 1990 she was working on a daytime programme called *Open Air* and was sent to make a behind-the-scenes film about the *Antiques Roadshow* when they were recording at Manchester Town Hall. She was so impressed with the set-up that when a vacancy arose for a director on the programme, she applied. She has been with the Roadshow ever since and became the producer in 1994.

Jessie Butler
reception

Jessie has been involved with the Roadshow since the first programme. Her working career started with ten years at the headquarters of J Sainsbury. Jessie is married to Roy Butler, and as a partner in her husband's auction house, Wallis and Wallis, she takes a prominent role at the fairs and shows that they attend in Europe and the United States. At the Roadshow, she ensures easy access for people in wheelchairs, the disabled and pregnant women; and helps to calm unhappy children, as excess noise needs to be avoided with the cameras running (a biscuit usually does the trick). She also keeps her eye on the various queues, making sure they do not become mixed, particularly in small venues.

John Curry
assistant to recording manager

John started his career as an actor when he auditioned for children's drama for BBC radio. He made many recordings, including being in a series for six years. He then moved to television and the theatre, appearing in drama and musicals and finally stage management. A humble role on a TV quiz programme, where he was bringing on the objects, saw him being offered the job as floor assistant on the *Antiques Roadshow*. This was in 1977, and he has been alternating as a floor assistant and assistant recording manager ever since.

Jeanne Darrington
recording manager

Jeanne began her working life in advertising, moving to headhunting, graphic design and fashion. She then changed direction with Nicholas Mitchell. He introduced her to the *Antiques Roadshow,* where she became a steward, and the *Great Antiques Hunt* with Gilly Goolden as a minder to the contestants. In 1997, the then producer Christopher Lewis asked her to try the daunting job of recording manager, which she has done ever since.

Liz Nicol
Production Manager

Liz joined the BBC as a secretary in the Natural History Unit in 1978. She booked flights all over the world for the crews and production teams of programmes such as *The World About Us* and *Wildlife on One.* In 1992, she joined the *Antiques Roadshow* and as the progamme grew so did Liz's role and she progressed to Production Manager. A new move is to sports programmes.

John Neal engineering
manager and lighting director

John is a chartered engineer who started with BBC News in 1969. He transferred to the Television Centre and then to BBC Plymouth, moving to the Outside Broadcast Department 20 years ago. In 1985 he had a new role at BBC Bristol as engineering manager. He has been with the Roadshow since 1986. He is married to Sue who helps to keep guests and experts supplied with teas, coffee and water.

Pete Rose
sound supervisor

Peter joined the BBC in 1962 as a technical operator, moving on to sound supervisor in 1969, working on the full range of TV programmes but specializing in music and light entertainment. He moved to BBC Bristol in 1979 where, from 1980, he worked on the *Antiques Roadshow*. He continued on the Roadshow while training as a Permanent Deacon in the Catholic Church, into which he was ordained in 1998.

Alec Yirrell
front-of-house manager

Alec trained as a physical education teacher before becoming a lecturer in professional studies at a college of education. His knowledge of antiques burgeoned when he and his wife restored their first cottage in Derbyshire. In 1980 he became a general antiques dealer in Bath. His main interest is in collectables, small silver, objects of vertu and toys. Alec has been involved with the Roadshow since the second series.

John Stables, Lorna James, Beth Missen

Beth is a recording engineer who worked on her first *Antiques Roadshow* in 1988 in Bournemouth and since then has worked on every series. John, also a recording engineer, is a recent member of the Roadshow team who in the course of his career has met such diverse figures as John Major and Bob Geldof. Lorna James is a graduate in media communications who works as production secretary for the Roadshow.

Camera and sound

The main unit

Among the formidable ranks of vehicles parked up alongside any Roadshow venue are the vans containing a bewildering array of camera and sound equipment, all vital to the success of the day.

Three cameras make up the main unit, which records the longer items that merit a variety of close-ups. Before leaving base, technical personnel check and re-check the contents, ensuring that every item is on board. One missing component could spell disaster!

Main-unit cameramen

The cameramen arrive by mid-afternoon on Wednesday, ready to unload the equipment, set it in position and check and re-check it. Any problems relating to sound and vision are ironed out at this stage with engineering manager John Neal. At approximately 5 p.m., a rehearsal takes place. Every position that the cameras will occupy is tested to ensure that no fire exits or other unsightly features appear in shot.

PSC unit

The PSC (portable single camera) unit consists of one cameraman, a sound recordist and an assistant. They arrive on the Tuesday afternoon to work with Michael Aspel around the location, filming local landmarks and the opening and closing sequences of the programme, which have been thoroughly researched by one of the directors.

The Roadshow now holds many more outside events in the grounds of large, stately homes. On the day, a second PSC unit is often used to capture the atmosphere as well as the shorter, more spontaneous recordings.

The director working with the PSC unit keeps a separate list of items to be recorded from that adhered to by the main unit. Throughout the day they move to different areas of the venue, taking advantage of a different variety of backgrounds both inside and out. Spare a thought for the cameraman who spends his entire working life with a heavy camera resting on his shoulder!

◀ **Two PSC units** were on hand to record events at this open-air Roadshow. Left to right: Jim Bolton (sound recordist), Hayley Sparke (production assistant), Joe Harrison (assistant to cameraman), Ian Stanley (cameraman), Merrick Simmonds (PSC director), John Hunter (cameraman), Richard Smith (assistant to cameraman), Nicola Lafferty (PSC director) and Phil Middleham (sound recordist).

▲ A great deal of physical strength as well as a good eye is required to meet the high standards required of a **BBC** cameraman. These main units are on wheels, but have to be hauled from the vehicles in sections, assembled and pulled to the camera positions, often over lawns and along gravel paths. At around 7 p.m. at the end of a long day, the process happens in reverse. Four cameramen work the main unit, so that each can take short breaks in the gruelling recording schedule. Left to right: **Bruce Miller, Richard North, Dave Fader and Brady Pollard.**

Making the programme

Ensuring that every member of the team and every piece of equipment arrives safely at every Roadshow venue is a daunting task. All of the different locations chosen for each series must be thoroughly researched in advance. By the time the public starts arriving on the day itself, every aspect of a site has been carefully considered and every potential technical problem anticipated and eliminated. Behind the scenes an experienced production team is on hand to deal with all aspects of the making of the programme, from its earliest planning stages, through the process of filming and editing, right up until the final tape is delivered to BBC headquarters in London and the programme is transmitted.

◀ **Expert Andrew Davis, a veteran of the Furniture Round, is filmed by the main camera unit discussing an English oak longcase clock with its owner, against the magnificent backdrop of Portmeirion village in North Wales.**

Planning the Roadshows

New series in the making

The relaxed atmosphere of the Roadshow disguises the meticulous planning that precedes each event. Filming takes place between April and November, but early in the year the shortlist of possible locations is finalized.

Suggestions are often sent in by members of the public. Experts also have a hand in the process, often contacting the team to say they have given a lecture or carried out a valuation day at a place that seems to fit the bill.

Filming alfresco

Increasingly, our beautiful stately homes and castles have become dazzling arenas for the Roadshow when filming takes place outside amid the topiary. In many instances, the owners or managers of these historic sites make the initial contact with the production office.

Nothing left to chance

Every feasible location is inspected by a member of the production team, who travel the length and breadth of the country, assessing size, ease of access, parking facilities and how many visitors a place might attract.

The dynamic duo known affectionately as "John and John", aka engineering manager John Neal and designer John Bone, then make their first technical reconnaissance. If all goes well, work begins to transform it into another successful location.

Reaching out

The Roadshow criss-crosses the country in the making of every series. The database is consulted for past locations and the trusty wall map pored over, the mission being to attract as many people as possible within a 40-km (25-mile) radius of the event. The *Antiques Roadshow* now has such a long history that inevitably towns and cities are being revisited, and the team always receives a warm welcome.

▶ **The Roadshow is coming! No matter how far and fast computer technology advances, the central feature of the programme's office remains the wall map, which is dotted with pins marking the locations for each series.**

Last-minute detail

Once the list is finalized, it goes out to everyone involved, including the all-important experts who tick the dates when they are available and return the list to Bristol where the team draw the up lists and decides which experts go where. As time goes on, the planning intensifies. Hotels are booked, travel arrangements made and local newspapers and radios stations contacted.

Six weeks before a Roadshow, with every detail attended to, a full production meeting takes place to anticipate and solve last-minute problems. Nothing is left to chance. By the time equipment, staff and experts are on site, several exhaustive weeks of planning are behind them.

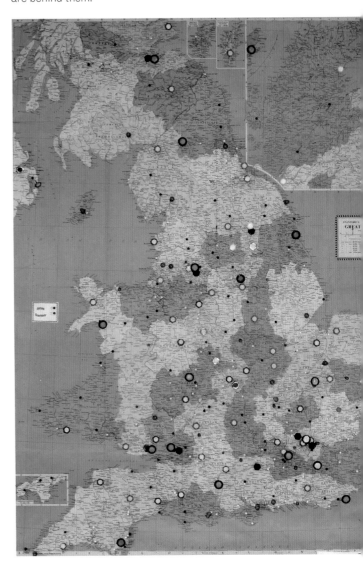

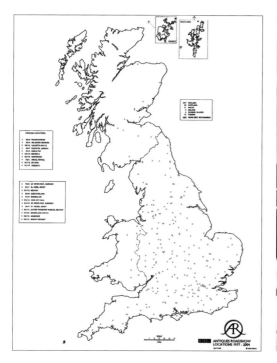

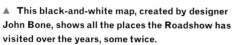

▲ This black-and-white map, created by designer John Bone, shows all the places the Roadshow has visited over the years, some twice.

▲ Production manager Liz Nicol (far right) presides over a formidable bank of folders holding vital information on each location.

▼ Series editor Simon Shaw (seated in front of map) gathers his team around him to bring them up to date on progress at venues around the country. He holds at least one major meeting a month.

Setting up at the location

The early light of Monday morning sees the first lorries rumble up to the location. A large, quiet space greets the team of scaffolders, who spend the day building the towers and arranging the network of poles across the roof space that allows the nimble lighting crew to do their job.

Lighting the space

On Tuesday morning the long task begins of rigging the dozens of heavy five-kilowatt tungsten lamps used to light the event. If you've ever stood for hours in the queue at a Roadshow, you'll have felt the oppressive heat they generate!

It takes 12 hours to hoist the lamps on pulleys to the top of the scaffolding towers. On the day, there is a specific lighting control for each camera position, with a console that allows the set-up to be driven from the on-site production room.

All hands on deck

By Tuesday afternoon, with only 24 hours to go, another crew is rigging the set and the scanner (the mobile control room) has arrived and parked up. Various teams work together with one objective – to complete the mammoth task of transforming the venue within the deadline. The layout of each Roadshow is the responsibility of designer John Bone, whilst engineering manager John Neal masterminds every technical aspect of the operation.

Final details

By Wednesday afternoon, the 65 or 70 screens, or "flats" as they are known, are slotted together inside the venue to create the "room" in which the Roadshow takes place. Outdoor events involve an entirely different scheme involving erecting marquees and setting up tables outside. The furniture arrives and front-of-house manager Alex Yirrell briefs local helpers who work as stewards for the day.

Series editor Simon Shaw gathers his production team about him to finalize last-minute details. By early evening, a tired but satisfied group of people retire for the night. The scene is set for another Roadshow.

▲ The large articulated lorry holding the set, carefully packed and ready for quick assembly, draws up at the location.

▶ Three miles of cable link the main unit cameras in the hall to the scanner (the mobile recording unit). For the children's roadshow, fifteen tonnes of cable are used for lights and cameras.

▲ During rehearsal, John Neal stands at his temporary desk to pre-programme the lighting computer for the broadcast day.

◄ The interior of the scanner with its impressive bank of monitors and switches where the director sits, relaying instructions to the cameramen on the main unit.

▼ Early Tuesday morning, and the lighting equipment is unloaded from the lorry before the crew begin rigging the dozens of five-kilowatt tungsten lamps needed to light the show. The large trunk-like pieces of apparatus are dimmer racks, each containing 36 dimmers.

◀ At the start of the rigging process, the team begin to attach each lamp to a strong pulley so that it can be hoisted to the top of the scaffolding tower. It can take up to 12 hours to complete the job.

▲ ▶ Meticulous planning and the pooling of different skills amongst the TVOs (television operatives) and riggers are vital to the success of the day. Left to right, back row: Barry Humphries, Kevin Parker, Clive Treacher, Stan Hamblen and Trevor Poole; sitting: John Wood, John Sweet, Rob Looker, Glenn Ivers and Andy Bishop.

▶ The distribution unit relays power from the mains (or the generator) to the dimmers and back again to each individual light.

◀ Experts and the production team look forward to the public arriving at a Roadshow held in Chichester Cathedral.

▼ Front-of-house manager Alec Yirrell briefs the team of stewards on Wednesday afternoon. All volunteers, they kindly offer their time to organize queues and provide refreshments on the day.

▲ Executive producer Simon Shaw discusses the furniture brought in by the lorry with expert Martin Levy (right) and other members of the production team.

▲ Series editor Simon Shaw stands to talk briefly to experts and production staff about the day ahead, as they all gather in the dining room of the hotel the night before.

Michael Aspel presents

Michael's witty, information-packed introduction at the beginning of every Roadshow gives us a rounded view of the location in a few short minutes. His relaxed delivery belies the weeks of research that precede those few hours spent filming on the day before the Roadshow, when the flavour of the place and its people are captured.

The team of directors works in rotation, researching the area and writing a script in a simple narrative style that allows the crew to move from one part of the location to another following a particular theme – and that's just the creative part! At this stage, access to various monuments or buildings is requested and a multitude of other practical considerations dealt with.

Michael's approval

The script is then sent to Michael who personalizes it, introducing his own sense of humour and suggesting various changes. Once the script is finalized, a schedule is drawn up so that as little time as possible is wasted on the day. The director takes into consideration how wide an area has to be covered. In a city, for instance, moving around in heavy traffic has to be built into the schedule, whereas if the Roadshow is taking place in the grounds of a stately home, the introduction may encompass only a few thousand square yards of house and gardens.

With few exceptions, the introduction is filmed on the day before the event. However, when preparations for the Roadshow spoil the overall look of the location, such as when a large marquee in front of a stately home obscures its grandeur, the schedule is adapted.

Michael records between three and six pieces to camera, each one involving two to three takes. All of the directors agree that he's good on the first take, but it's considered foolhardy not to do a second and often a third. Michael also often asks to do a piece again to satisfy his own high standards. The final part of the introduction is completed on the morning of the Roadshow. By then the queues are growing and Michael is recorded as the event gathers momentum.

Goodbye

It is mid- to late- afternoon when Michael, the director, and the executive producer Simon Shaw get together to discuss how the day has gone. Michael then writes his closing script, perhaps referring to the people he has met, the weather and, of course, the surprises and stories that have captured his imagination.

▲ **Cameraman Guy Littlemore records Michael's complimentary thoughts on the Roadshow held at Tyntesfield, the National Trust's Gothic Revival mansion in north Somerset, once home to the Gibbs family, wealthy industrialists in the nineteenth century.**

▲ Michael listens to his own voice
on playback while watching the
recording he has just made on a
12.5-cm (5-in) square colour
monitor linked to the camera.
Director Simon Pass (left) and
cameraman John Hunter (right)
wait for his comments.

▶ The PSC (portable single
camera) unit records Michael's
farewell after a successful
Roadshow in the grounds
of Hampton Court Palace.

The furniture round

▲ ▲ **Nicholas Mitchell takes a first look at the bulging furniture file; his task to whittle it down to around 60 entries involving 20 visits each day.**

▲ **Nicholas watches as the removal men carefully carry a sideboard down steps to the waiting lorry. Once loaded, it will be wrapped for safe transport.**

Publicity is vital

Six weeks before a Roadshow, advertising ensures that as many people as possible know of the team's imminent arrival. Posters, as well as local television and radio, spread the news, inviting those with objects too heavy to carry to write in or email photographs and descriptions, all of which are considered and collated in a file.

The expert takes over

On the Friday before the event, one of the team of furniture specialists arrives in the area with an assistant producer or director, and is handed the weighty file. The painstaking process of choosing enough eye-catching pieces of furniture, clocks, sculpture, paintings and other objects for designer John Bone to arrange on the set begins.

The expert's eye is often caught by interesting and valuable objects that the owners have never thought worth considering. The verdict on their true worth is, of course, never revealed until the day of filming.

For the next three days, as many as 60 visits are made to homes within a 40-km (25-mile) radius of the location. Before the advent of the mobile telephone, it was a tricky juggling act with appointments made the previous day from the hotel. Even today, the hotel room is an important focus, doubling up as office and makeshift headquarters for the week. Decision time.

By Tuesday morning it's time to make a final choice of objects to be collected by the removals firm. Owners are contacted and arrangements finalized. Tough decisions have to be made. Pieces are often rejected simply because they fall outside a route that will allow collections to be made in one day.

Collection day

Early on Wednesday morning the circuitous round of collections begins, with the furniture expert riding in the cab of the furniture lorry and the assistant producer following in a car. Whatever obstacles they encounter, they aim to arrive at the location by 4 p.m. with a full load and with each piece carefully wrapped and handled.

As the lorry is unloaded, the expert discusses the selection of furniture and other objects with series editor Simon Shaw. Once they have decided which of the pieces are good enough to film, the set builders begin to create the backdrop display.

By Friday evening, the process has been carried out in reverse. Every object is back in place and a relieved expert sets off for home.

▶ **Safely arrived!** The removal men begin taking off some of the polystyrene-packed objects and furniture, before carrying it into the hall. The process will be reversed on Friday morning.

▼ The **TVOs** (television operatives) who build the set follow the lengthy procedure of unpacking all the furniture and objects so that they can be examined and assessed.

◀ The day's work is collected together in one area before designer John Bone begins the creative process of arranging it. Other aspects of the set can be planned in advance, but John must act spontaneously according to what is unloaded from the lorry.

▲ Expert George Archdale carefully puts back together all the components of a longcase clock disassembled for transport. The expert often gets involved in handling more delicate pieces.

On the day

An early start

There is no sight more gratifiying than a healthy queue beginning to form in the early morning light. It marks the start of a long, tiring, but thoroughly enjoyable day for the public, the experts and all those who work tirelessly behind the scenes. At St. Ives in 2004 the first customer had camped out all night, and it is not uncommon for people to be found patiently waiting at 7 a.m.

The set is complete, the technical and design details have been fine-tuned, the Reception staff are ready and the stewards have been briefed. An atmosphere of tension and anticipation prevails. The success of every event is now firmly in the hands of the public.

The cameras roll

Filming starts promptly at 9.30 a.m., usually with a select number of items brought in with the furniture the day before. The first wave of customers comes onto the set to create the bustling atmosphere that is an essential part of the Roadshow.

For the rest of the day the momentum builds and filming continues with directors and camera crew working in rotation. While the happily milling throng may look chaotic, it is underpinned by an impressive calm maintained by meticulous organization.

Behind the scenes

If you've ever wondered why you have to step over so many cables at a Roadshow, it's because they lead off the set and into the scanner, the lorry which acts as the mobile recording unit. In here, a director gives instructions to the floor manager via an earpiece, and the sound supervisor and vision engineers record sound and look after the colour and contrast on the camera exposures.

A production room is also set up, usually just off the set, where the proceedings can be viewed on a range of monitors. The staff in here can talk to those in the scanner at the flick of a switch.

The recording schedule

Recording manager Jeanne Darrington keeps an iron grip on the schedule, ensuring that customers, their objects and the experts are in front of the camera on time.

Needless to say, pieces are never discussed with the owner before a recording, in case a vital scrap of information slips out prematurely and spoils the moment of revelation.

Stars of Reception

Those on Reception unwrap and examine objects, issue tickets for relevant queues and keep smiling! They are often the first point of contact for customers, and without their diligence and unfailing good humour the day could not run smoothly.

◀ ▼ **It's the early bird that catches the worm. Some of the team of experts arrive at the Roadshow at the start of what promises to be a long and busy day.**

▼ **The patience of Roadshow visitors is legendary. A typically lengthy queue snakes its way through the shrubbery from early morning well into the afternoon.**

◄ Front-of-house manager Alec Yirrell directs members of the public towards Reception.

▼ The eccentric choice of wrapping materials has always been a colourful feature of the Roadshow. A customer arrives with her worldly goods strapped to a luggage trolley.

▲ A wise member of the public arrives with a precious painting carefully wrapped in lengths of protective fabric.

► On Reception, Rosamund Hinds-Howell looks at a customer's offerings, dispenses tickets and explains the queuing system.

▲ A recording is about to begin. The mysterious object has arrived on set in its straw packing, where it has remained for fourty years, and **D**avid **B**attie begins to lift it carefully onto the table, closely watched by the anxious owners.

◄ So that's where all the supermarket trolleys disappear to! A customer unwraps her substantial haul that has been wheeled all the way from home in complete safety.

◄ ◄ A day in the garden or a day at the Roadshow? A wheelbarrow must be one of the most original objects that has ever been used to transport treasures.

▲ Messages on old postcards are a great source of amusement and social history. Hilary Kay and Tim Wonnacott shares a droll moment.

▼ Ceramics experts Gordon Lang and Fergus Gambon discuss an ornate suite of hand-painted miniature porcelain furniture.

▶ Bunny Campione is enthralled by this rare set of miniature horn and ivory Anglo-Indian furniture, beautifully preserved under a glass dome and inherited by the owner from his grandfather.

◀ **Arms and Armour expert Bill Harriman** knows a thing or two about antique firearms and swords. He explains all to an enthusiastic collector keen to share his passion.

▶ **Clock expert Richard Price** points to the detail in the floral marquetry on this longcase clock with its impressive brass dial.

▶ **Recording manager Jeanne Darrington** (centre) discusses the schedule with books expert **Clive Farahar** (left) and a customer (right).

▼ **Recording manager Jeanne Darrington** (left) and her assistant **Roma Hussey** (right) plan the next records with series editor **Simon Shaw**, who keeps a close eye on all aspects of the event.

◀ The make-up lady is vital to the success of the day. No shiny noses allowed! Every customer waiting to be recorded is given a minor makeover before being called.

▶ One of the sound engineers gently fits a microphone to a customer before she is filmed.

▶▶ Miscellaneous expert Hilary Kay is delighted to explain the wonderful detail on this unusual and highly desirable German tinplate ship.

◀ As the camera rolls, Hugo Morley Fletcher discusses the merits of an interesting jug and explains the type of decoration to the owner.

▲ Large and impressive collections have become a feature of the Roadshow. Michael Aspel admires a much-treasured array of acoustic guitars that are owned by an accomplished musician.

▼ The jimmy jib is a camera on the end of a long arm used to provide stylish, sweeping shots of the locations. It's often used for Michael Aspel's pieces to camera for the introduction and closing sequences or for crowd shots and links between experts' sequences.

▼ ◀ Main unit cameraman Brady Pollard surveys the Roadshow set through his lens.

◀ Clock and watch expert Richard Price closely examines a fine, small gold pocket watch.

▶ During every recording on the main unit, series editor Simon Shaw sits behind monitors and listens on a set of headphones. He then discusses the content and style and is able to ask for changes and retakes on the spot, until he has a flow and a storyline that he feels happy with.

▲ PSC (portable single camera) sound recordist Phil Middleham fits a microphone to a customer.

▶ Long-time Roadshow fan Averil Beresford sports her homemade waistcoat adorned with the autographs of all the experts, each one edged with sequins.

▶ ▶ Rain never stops play! But a black waterproof sheet helps immensely when trying to view a monitor during a cloud burst.

◀ Ceramics expert John Sandon enjoys a lively discussion with a customer who has brought in two Berlin painted-porcelain plaques to show him.

▼ ◀ Where better to show off a monumental painted Chinese pot than at an outside event? Lars Tharp explains the technical problems involved in throwing large pots to a fascinated owner.

▼ What an amazing spread! Jewellery expert Geoffrey Munn is suitably impressed by the quantity and variety of this woman's jewellery collection.

◀ Michael Aspel takes the trouble to spend part of each Roadshow autographing various objects for his many fans.

▲ What better way to view the excitement of the Roadshow than in this bird's eye view of the event as it unfolds?

◀ ▼ Few visitors leave the Roadshow without a visit to the shop, where mugs, tea towels, bookmarks and T-shirts make ideal souvenirs of the day.

▼ One of the bestselling items in the shop are the postcards featuring presenter Michael Aspel, a snip at only 50p each.

Editing the programme

Miles of tape

The team leaves every Roadshow with a pile of videotapes holding many hours' worth of material, including 50 items recorded by the main and PSC (portable single camera) units, Michael Aspel's introduction and a variety of scenic footage. The editing process will shrink these rich pickings to between 18 and 20 items, each no longer than two to four minutes, to create the lively, 45-minute programme. Some of the unusual items go into compilations.

Cutting to fit

The first highly labour-intensive stage lasts three to four days. All the material is viewed and detailed notes are made. Each tape shows a digital timecode at the edge of the screen so exact sections can be identified.

Two weeks are then spent in the off-line edit suite, dipping in and out of footage, selecting scenes and making necessary cuts. It is during this second stage that the basic programme takes shape, using fast and efficient computers with a digital copy of the footage stored on disk.

At this point, series editor Simon Shaw views the first cut and discussions take place about which items should be dropped and which saved for one of the special compilation programmes.

Fine tuning

The VT (videotape) editor begins the highly skilled process of creating a seamless recording. A picture-perfect programme emerges, complete with opening titles and credits, but imperfect sound. At this point, the programme goes to dubbing for the sound to be improved.

Crowd noise is added, and unwanted sounds such as excessive coughing or babies crying are taken out.

Finishing touches

The remaining vital stage is "layback," where the new sound is laid back onto the transmission tape. This is the last opportunity to correct any tiny flaws, and the team crowd around the monitors to watch and take notes. Perfection finally achieved, the tape is signed and dispatched to BBC Television Centre in London for transmission.

◀ **Proof of many years of success lies on the shelves of this room at the Television Centre in Bristol, where copies of every *Antiques Roadshow* since the first programme was transmitted in 1977 are stored.**

▶ **Videotape editors and directors work together during the off-line edit, when the footage is cut to exactly the right length.**

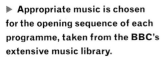

▲ The so-called "paper edit" takes place here, when a director views the tapes and suggests possible cuts.

▶ Appropriate music is chosen for the opening sequence of each programme, taken from the **BBC**'s extensive music library.

The Roadshow abroad

International appeal

A successful television formula will attract the attention of programme makers throughout the world. Small wonder, then, that the *Antiques Roadshow,* with its soaring ratings, was closely studied from its inception by producers in various countries. In the late 1980s the then executive producer, Christopher Lewis, was approached by Swedish television executives and a deal was struck with Sweden and Denmark. These, the first two programmes to be made abroad, were recorded in 1989 and included in series 12.

Triumphs abroad

Negotiations soon began with other countries. Programmes have since been recorded in Jamaica, Gibraltar, Brussels, Arras in France, Dublin and Cork in Ireland, Amsterdam in the Netherlands and Ottawa and Toronto in Canada. A mini-Roadshow was even held in Japan, attended by just three experts (see below right). The response in every country has been overwhelmingly positive.

The odd hiccup

Logistics and practicalities are always important issues for the Roadshow team. The pressure to ensure nothing goes wrong with equipment or planning is even greater when they are abroad. The best way to avoid difficulties and misunderstandings is to employ a trustworthy local "fixer" who can spot a problem before it happens. Even so, the best-laid plans …

Language barrier

Language posed no problem in Malta, Gibraltar, Jamaica or Canada, but in Amsterdam, Arras and Brussels the team had their first experience of interpreting by earpiece. There were slight pauses, but they were edited out later and the system was declared a great success. The Roadshow has always to be recorded in English for the British audience. Many countries want the Roadshow to visit, but for the programme to be recorded in their own language. Sadly, their requests have to be declined. Happily, the speed of technology allows many problems to be overcome. This means that there may be many more overseas Roadshows peppering the schedule in future series.

▼ **St John's Hospital, Valetta, built by the Knights of St John at the end of the sixteenth century, provided a splendidly imposing setting for the Roadshow held in Malta in 1990. The experts were presented with an impressive array of fascinating objects brought in by an enthusiastic crowd.**

▼ **The poster produced to publicize the mini-Roadshow mounted by Japan's largest television company in the mid-1990s, when Hilary Kay, Rupert Maas and Henry Sandon travelled to Tokyo. All conversations required a translator and all were conducted with customary Japanese formality and ceremony.**

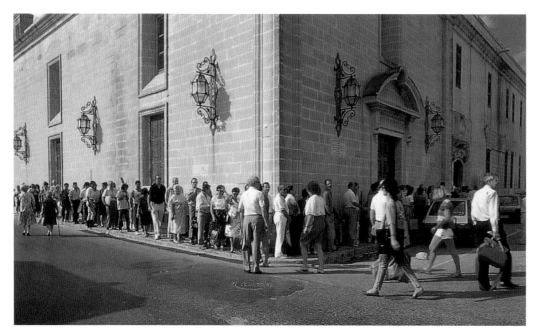

Not least among the items brought along to the event in Malta were several stunning pieces of jewellery, including this wide, solid-gold bangle. The piece is decorated with circular micro-mosaic panels, showing peasant figures, set into plaques of malachite.

◄ The weather was balmy and the scenic locations abundant. Hugh Scully stands at the water's edge in Malta to record a piece to camera. The island, 58 miles southwest of Sicily and filled with Baroque architecture, has long been a magnet for the British.

◄ Negotiating the narrow streets of Malta, which are lined with stone houses containing a wealth of fine pictures and furniture, proved tricky. The lorry eventually arrived at the location, where local helpers unloaded the furniture and pictures stowed inside.

▲ As the sun began to set behind the great rock of Gibraltar, the lorry containing the set – resplendent with the unmistakable logo of the *Antiques Roadshow* – arrived safely at this southernmost tip of Europe.

◀ These houses among the treetops in the Philippines are the subject matter of another of the Lozano watercolours (see right). The owner's grandfather, who commissioned the paintings, owned a cigar factory in Manila.

▶ This depiction of a group of rather dapper gentlemen is just one of the 25 watercolours by the artist José Honorato Lozano that were found by Peter Nahum at Brussels. They were in an album of valuable Filipino paintings that was later sold at auction, through Christie's, for the remarkable sum of £250,000.

◀ People came from all over the island to Jamaica's Roadshow, the furthest afield that the team has ventured. They were given a warm welcome during several memorable days under Caribbean skies.

▲ It was a busy day at Reception – and a sweltering one, too, as the crowds thronged the open-air venue at Devon House in Kingston, Jamaica, for the fourth successful overseas event.

◄ It took seven years to organize a co-production with CBC Newsworld to make a Canadian Roadshow, but it did eventually take place in 2001. Ottawa and Toronto were the two centres and the sites of the longest queues in the history of the programme. Some hopefuls telephoned over 100 times. Because of the massive response, tickets had to be issued. Here in Ottawa, Clive Stewart-Lockhart, Paul Atterbury, Alastair Dickenson, Rupert Maas and Mark Poltimore discuss where they will eat out on the day before the recording.

► A view of the queue at the National Gallery, Ottawa. People came from all over Canada to the two shows, some flying nearly 5,000km (over 3,000 miles).

◄ The mock-Gothic castle, Casa Loma, in Toronto where the Roadshow was held. As the response in Ottawa had been so overwhelming, extra Canadian experts were arranged at the last minute for Toronto.

▲ A photograph of the only appearance of a Fortuny dress (valued at £2,000/c.$3,500) on a Roadshow. By chance, David Battie's sixteen-year-old daughter Eleanor was in Amsterdam and was co-opted into a modelling job.

▲ ◀ **David Battie** discusses a superb Japanese silver pheasant incense burner with a client who was too late to be recorded in **Ottawa**, so waited three days and turned up in **Toronto**. He was given the first record of the day there.

◀ **Roy Butler**, in a straw hat to ward off the hot **Canadian** sun, unsheathes a sword against the appropriate backdrop of **Casa Loma, Toronto**.

▲ **Henry Sandon** expounding on his favourite subject, **Royal Worcester**, in **Toronto**, a home-from-home for him, as he had for a while been curator of the **George R Gardiner Museum** there.

▼ **The Roadshow** team setting up in the brilliantly lit hall of the **National Gallery of Ottawa** the day before the public appeared.

▲ ▲ Mark Poltimore with a giant silkscreen print of Chairman Mao by Andy Warhol, one of the most unexpected finds in Ottawa.

◄ John Bly unravels the history of a drop-leaf oak table that was brought to the Ottawa Roadshow. Behind him is the "set" of furniture that arrived by carrier the night before.

▲ The full complement of experts and the then producer, Christopher Lewis, outside the National Gallery, Ottawa. All who went there dream of a return visit.

The Next Generation

Children's entertainment

BBC1 has always had a enviable reputation for its fast-moving Saturday morning children's programme, with its stream of guests, comedy acts and audience participation. It has gone through various incarnations but in the early 1990s it was called *Going Live*. The presenters at the time were Philip Schofield and Sarah Greene.

One celebrity guest during this period was the *Antiques Roadshow*'s Hilary Kay, who in her role as head of Sotheby's Collectors' Division brought along a selection of rock and pop memorabilia to show the audience.

New idea

The response to Hilary's appearance was overwhelming and the producers at *Going Live* began talking enthusiastically to their counterparts on the Roadshow in Bristol. They discussed putting on a children's show that would encourage young people's interest in collecting. Ask any number of the experts on the Roadshow when they began to appreciate antiques and you'll find they started at an early age, squirrelling away drawers full of stamps, conkers, coins and cigarette cards.

Established event

The children's shows are now an annual event, each taking place at an unusual venue with attractions to hold the attention of the children and provide an entertaining action-packed day out for the family. A celebrity presenter, well known to children everywhere, works with Michael Aspel throughout the day.

Entry by ticket

Unlike the *Antiques Roadshow,* where the public often queue for several hours, the children's shows are ticketed and divided into morning and afternoon sessions to minimize waiting. When the forthcoming event is advertised nationally, children who respond are sent application forms so that the production team have an idea of what will be coming in. There is greater emphasis on collections put together by the children themselves than on the value of individual items.

The children's enthusiasm for the event is infectious and thoroughly refreshing for the experts, who enjoy talking to visitors who are less concerned with the value of their collections than with the fun of putting them together.

▲ ▲ **Elaine Binning and a young collector of cigarette cards discuss his album, watched by his family. While the adults are allowed to listen in, any direct input is frowned on. This is a day for the collectors of the future.**

▲ **A young producer learns the ropes beside Simon Shaw, who is checking a recording by David Battie on the monitor. The *Next Generation Antiques Roadshow* gives children an insight into how an outside broadcast is made, and working the camera is an occasional treat.**

▲ A view of the Thinkspace Hall at the Millennium Point in Birmingham, where the *Next Generation Antiques Roadshow* was held on 14 November 2004. Children and their parents are beginning to filter into the recording space amongst the display of vintage and veteran cars.

◄ Rapt attention on the faces of two girls who had a marvellous group of jewellery between them, as they listen to John Benjamin during the recording.

◄ David Battie enthuses about a stuffed three-thousand-year-old crocodile to a budding Egyptologist who had inherited the specimen from her grandfather when doing a project on ancient Egypt. Unsure whether it was authentic, she had had it X-rayed. David thought that it might be worth several hundreds of pounds.

Frequently asked questions

The BBC *Antiques Roadshow* office in Bristol gets hundreds of letters and emails a week from devoted followers of the programme. While they are unable to answer any questions on antiques or collections, they are very keen to hear from viewers with any comments they may have. Like many of my Roadshow colleagues, I travel the country giving talks for antiques societies, charities, and cruises – and there is often a question-and-answer session. Here are the most Frequently Asked Questions.
David Battie

Can I take photographs on the day?

Yes and no. Film cameras are sensitive beasts and hate flashes so these are banned, but otherwise, yes. For complex copyright reasons, videos cannot be used.

How do I know where and when it's on?

The locations are listed in *Homes & Antiques* magazine, there is local information in newspapers and radio and you can check recording locations on the Roadshow website at www.bbc.co.uk/antiques.

Do the experts ever make mistakes?

Despite evidence to the contrary, experts are not perfect and – yes – now and again, we make mistakes. Most of these are picked up during the record and we re-record that section. We are also given tapes of our recordings on the day and can review these at home. Any small blunder, such as saying nineteenth century instead of eighteenth century, can often be lost in the cutting room – or occasionally with electronic scissors and tape, the correct words can be dropped in from elsewhere.

Is it rehearsed?

No rehearsal. Once the object is selected and the client and experts are miked up, the cameras are in position and off they go. The client has no idea at all what the expert is going to say, good or bad.

Do they ever drop anything?

I've already said we're not perfect! Very, very rarely does an accident happen. Most crashes on the day are caused by careless owners, but once in a blue moon the expert is responsible. After grovelling apologies from the perpetrator and then the producer, compensation is agreed and the piece restored. But, please, don't think this is common. It's rarer than Geoffrey Munn turning up a bit of Fabergé. One of the best remembered Roadshow moments was my smashing two "£50,000 [c.$92,000] Chinese famille-rose Buddhist lions" belonging to a nine-year-old girl. Of course, it was a set-up for *Jim'll Fix It* and, for me, who spends my life trying not to break things – very unnerving.

Why do some of the experts have dirty fingernails?

Along with Hugo Morley-Fletcher, I hold the record for the number of letters from disgruntled viewers appalled at the state of our fingernails. Hugo is a dedicated gardener and I periodically stain myself with leather dye when bookbinding – all too obvious in close up. Sorry.

Do the experts wear make-up?

We work mostly in sports halls with the air conditioning turned off because of the noise. The huge lights suspended above us pump out enough heat to prevent the entire population of the country suffering hypothermia over the winter period. Result: we glow; cure: make-up. Some of us need more than others ...

How many days does it take to shoot one Roadshow?

A Roadshow is recorded on one day at any location, but quite often there is enough material to make two programmes, or unused material can be utilized in compilation shows.

Why don't the public always react? Do they know the price beforehand?

No, as above they are told nothing. There are two reasons for the non-appearance of the more usual "Oh no! I can't believe it!" One is the British stiff upper lip (it might be considered vulgar to appear over excited), and the other is shock. Sitting down in front of three cameras with a well-known TV face and surrounded by onlookers can be very daunting and the price may be the ultimate shock. The result: rigidity, often until the cameras are off, when there is total meltdown.

Can the experts buy the pieces?

The BBC is extremely protective of its good name and forbids (quite rightly) any links, financial or otherwise, between the experts and the clients. No cards, no names, no addresses: in fact, an expert's contract would be terminated for a violation.

Are the experts employed full time by the BBC?

The experts are drawn from auction houses and dealerships, or they are consultants. They are employed on a programme-by-programme basis, in most cases between six and ten days a year.

Don't I run a risk of burglary if I have my object shown on the Roadshow?

There has never been a single case of a burglary linked to an *Antiques Roadshow*. Your name and address are never given out on a programme, and are only known only to a limited number of BBC staff (not the experts). The programme is also recorded several months in advance of showing so there is no way a burglar can tie you up with your object. There are also police in the hall and in the car park. You can sleep easy.

Can I write to the experts for advice?

I'm afraid that for the reason given above, contact with the experts is not possible.

How long do I have to queue?

This is very much in the lap of the gods. A biting wind and rain can reduce queuing time to nil. Afternoons tend to be lighter than mornings, cities tend to be busier than the country. Record queuing times were Broxbourne and the Canada shows, exceeding eight hours.

How many people sell their pieces after they have seen the experts?

The answer is we don't and cannot know. If clients decide on the spot to sell, they are referred to the producer who gives them a range of options, from local dealers or auctions to the London salerooms. Sometimes one spots an object that has been on a Roadshow, but not often. I suspect that most people pass the object down to the next generation.

Is the Roadshow broadcast in other countries?

It is broadcast in (amongst other countries) Japan, Australia, South America, New Zealand, the USA, East Africa and Canada.

Does any other country make its own Roadshow?

There are unlicensed versions in a couple of European countries, and the United States and now Canada make their own, hugely popular, versions.

Memorable Finds

Over the years the Roadshow has asked the nation to turn out its broom cupboards, attics and garden sheds. The public has obliged and the rewards have been rich and plentiful. Some of these treasures have been groundbreaking and they have included fabulous works of art thought to have been lost. Others have simply delighted experts by their beauty or quirkiness. Some have changed the lives of their owners, who considered them worthless and of little merit until the magical moment when, as the cameras rolled, the truth was revealed. On the following pages you can read about some of the memorable finds that stick in the minds of the experts long after the day of the event.

◀ **Henry Sandon, one of the longest serving and best loved of all *Antiques Roadshow* experts, shares his admiration of Worcester blue-and-white painted porcelain with a visitor who arrived with a collection of mugs and jugs.**

Cold-painted bronze parrot

Found at Newport, Isle of Wight, 1997. Valued at £4,000 (c.$7,500).

Eric Knowles is always quick to recognize the "Wow" factor when he comes into contact with it, and he spotted this life-size bird from a distance at a Roadshow in the Isle of Wight.

"Strictly speaking, this is a scarlet macaw and a stunning one at that!," he told the owner whose father bought it in London in 1924. "He's so well modelled he looks as if he might take off across the hall at any moment! I know the signature – immediately recognizable as that of Franz Bergman, the best-known sculptor producing these very distinctive cold-painted bronzes in Vienna at the beginning of the twentieth century."

The majority of Bergman bronzes are much smaller than this, Eric pointed out. "I have seen smaller birds modelled life-size by Bergman, such as blackbirds and woodpeckers, but never a macaw like this."

Bergman was a prolific artist. Apart from his huge range of small animals and Arab figure groups, he also produced figural lamps modelled as Bedouin leading camels, and these occasionally come up for auction. After the pieces emerged from the mould they were painted in oils, but the pigments were not then fired to fuse them to the body. Consequently, the paint has a tendency to flake over time.

"I'm delighted to see that this handsome bird has enjoyed a caring home," Eric concluded. "The colours are still strong and fresh, which adds to the bird's value."

Franz Bergman marks

Bergman bronzes are not always marked, but those that are feature a small, twin-handled amphora-like vessel centred with a "B." He also produced a widely sought-after range of tastefully erotic subjects (see page 134) and these are often signed "NAMGREB," which is his own name spelt backwards.

Ozzy the Owl

Found in Northampton, 1989. Valued at over £20,000 (c.$37,000) and sold at Phillips in 1990 to the Potteries Museum and Art Gallery, Stoke-on-Trent for £22,000 (c.$40,800). Current value £30–40,000 (c.$55,700–74,000).

Occasionally a Roadshow discovery causes such a stir that it hits the headlines. So it was with "Ozzy the Owl," a Staffordshire slipware drinking pot, c.1685–90, whose rarity and charm captured the hearts of the nation. As the owner unwrapped the layers of newspaper surrounding the piece, Henry Sandon knew exactly what he was looking at. "Staffordshire slipware is one of the earliest identifiable types of pottery made in the area, and its production had more or less ceased by the beginning of the eighteenth century," he said. "Surviving pieces are very desirable, but this little drinking pot – the body would have been used as the jug and the separate head as the cup – was in feathered slipware, which is even rarer. An ordinary mug would have been an exciting find, but the figures, like Ozzy, are rarer still, so he really was a very important discovery." The owl had been in the owner's family for many years and was used, with the cover removed, as a flower vase.

About ten owls have turned up in total, according to Henry – probably all made by the same person. He thinks that the maker simply loved owls and produced these cups as amusing little objects. They were made in rather a soft earthenware covered with a lead glaze, and were never meant to last for a long time. The decoration was made by putting coloured slip (liquid clay) onto the body of the pot and then feathering it with a quill before firing. The pieces were then dipped into a lead glaze and fired again.

Ozzy's owner had travelled by bus to the Roadshow, but so immediate was the interest surrounding the discovery that the BBC sent her home in a taxi accompanied by two policemen, much to her mother's consternation when she opened the door. After the piece was sold the owner told Henry that she had used the money to adopt five orphans from around the world. Ozzy now lives in a custom-built cabinet in the Potteries Museum and Art Gallery, Stoke-on-Trent – a special home for a very important owl.

Staffordshire slipware

The feathering used to decorate Ozzy is uncommon outside the Staffordshire potteries. They made pieces for ordinary domestic purposes using a red or buff-coloured clay and decorated the pieces in brown and cream slip (liquid clay). Once applied and while still wet, the slip was drawn through with a quill to "feather" the pattern, just as on marbled paper.

Bear claret jug

Found in Ludlow, 1996. Valued at £5–10,000 (c.$9–18,000) and later sold for £25,000 (c.$45,800).

The owner of this rare bear claret jug inherited it from his mother only two years before it was brought to the Roadshow by his wife. Little did she realize how much excitement it would cause.

"I've seen many a Victorian novelty claret jug," said expert Ian Pickford, "but I've never seen a bear before. It was an amazing example of inventive and imaginative Victorian silver. Claret jugs began to be made at the end of the eighteenth century but had become extremely fashionable by the mid-nineteenth. This example was made in 1875."

Rare survivor

The vast majority of claret jugs are of glass with silver mounts, and even the novelty examples have glass bodies (see page 110). Examples like this in solid silver are extremely rare, despite being far less vulnerable to breakage. The rich texture of the body was achieved with chasing, that is by working the surface of the silver with a hammer or a punch to create the desired design in relief, in this case the texture of the bear's fur. The wine was poured through his mouth and the head pulls off. Unlike other jugs, there was no handle; the body had to be grasped firmly for pouring!

Robert Hennell IV (1826–92)

The jug was made by Robert Hennell IV, one member of the famous and long-lived family firm of London silversmiths who started by making salt cellars in the eighteenth century. The company, still in business as Hennell jewellers in Bond Street, is thought to be one of the oldest family-run businesses in London. The dynasty began with David Hennell I who was apprenticed to Edward Wood in 1728, made free in 1735, and entered his first mark in 1736. He had 15 children, only five of whom reached maturity. Robert IV, the maker of this jug, employed his wife and nine men in the business, which moved from Northumberland Street to Charlotte Street just before the bear was made.

Paul Storr salt cellars

Found in Salisbury, 1990. Valued at £40,000 (c.$74,000) and sold for £66,000 (c.$122,000).

This remarkably rare set of four salt cellars by the foremost Regency silversmith Paul Storr now forms part of the important collection of silver at the Salters' Company in the City of London.

The owner brought one of them to the Roadshow in a brown paper bag, believing it to be made of brass. Penny Brittain spotted the maker's mark and sent him home for the other three. After several nail-biting hours, he turned up with them very late in the day, recorded as the last item.

The owner explained that his parents had been in service and were given them as a retirement present. He had kept them in a plastic bag at the bottom of a cupboard since he had inherited them. Modelled as shells held aloft by mermaids, and mermen, three were made in 1813 and the other in 1811.

Paul Storr (1771–1844)

Paul Storr first registered his mark at Goldsmiths' Hall in 1792, shortly afterwards joining the renowned firm of Rundell & Bridge. He was later a partner in the company that became Rundell Bridge and Rundell in 1805. He was most active between 1797 and 1821, when he was involved in the making of important pieces for clients such as King George III and the Prince Regent. He left the company in 1821 and went into partnership with John Mortimer before retiring in 1839.

Chinese stamp

Discovered at the Science Museum, 1993. Valued at £5,000 (c.$9,000).

Chinese stamps

With the modern-day wealth in China, nearly every major collection of Chinese stamps is now held there. The Chinese postal service is one of the oldest in the world and was talked about in admiring terms by Marco Polo after his return from the East in the late thirteenth century.

This extremely rare China 1885 3 Candarins stamp was brought to a Children's Roadshow by a young man who had been given his stamp album by a great aunt and was spotted by expert Tony Banwell who trawled through hundreds of albums on the day.

The number "3" in each bottom corner was put in as an experiment before the smaller version of this stamp came out. After the Roadshow, several more came to light and it is thought that one sheet of 25 stamps was released with the same flaw.

The find caused such a stir on the international market that it became known by philatelists everywhere as the "South Kensington Small 3", making £5,700 (c.$10,500) at Sotheby's in 1994.

Viennese enamel cornucopia

Found at Cliveden, 2000. Valued at £10,000–15,000 (c.$18–27,500).

The densely and beautifully decorated enamel work produced by a variety of workshops in Vienna during the nineteenth century is appreciated and collected all over the world. Lars Tharp was delighted to come across this example of staggering quality, inherited by the owner from her father, a collector of antiques.

The cornucopia

"The cornucopia or 'horn of plenty' is a very complicated shape to make," Lars explained, "This was modelled as a drinking horn but was never intended to be put to any practical use. It's very much a cabinet piece and you can see why. The decoration was inspired by the Renaissance and is quite exquisite.

"We can see Orpheus, the god of music, dragging Eurydice out of Hades," explained Lars, "as well as other great classical scenes interspersed with dense floral bands in these very typical pinks, yellows and blues and with each of the sections mounted in silver."

Typical decoration

The decoration on this elegant horn was inspired by the Renaissance (the period from the early fourteenth to the late sixteenth century) and the cornucopia or "horn of plenty" is also very much a motif of that period, often held by the god Ceres and brimming with tumbling fruit and flowers. Cornucopias were also made in pottery and porcelain, and made as wall pockets designed to hold flowers.

Rare Viennese enamel

Lars has examined many pieces of Viennese enamel over the years, but had never before come across such a feature as the silver horse of the sea elegantly draped over the plinth. "I think this is the most striking aspect of the whole piece, a real little sculpture in its own right!", he enthused.

L S Lowry painting

Found at Oldham, 1999. Valued in excess of £100,000 (c.$184,000).

Many fake Lowry paintings have found their way onto the market, but Stephen Somerville was convinced this one was "right" when it was brought to the Roadshow by a friend of the 79-year-old owner.

The picture belonged to the owner's late wife, who lived near the artist and was his chauffeur after he retired. She stopped driving for him after her marriage, but they remained friendly and he gave her the painting in 1957.

It was accompanied by a pencil sketch signed by Lowry on the inside of a cigarette packet, also given to the owner, who dissuaded Lowry from throwing it out of the car window and asked him to sign it. The provenance was good enough to leave no doubt in Stephen's mind about the painting's authenticity.

Unrecorded canvas

The painting was dated 1937 and had never been exhibited. Lowry was 50 years old when he finished it and was still relatively unknown as an artist, his enormous success still to come after an exhibition held at the Lefevre Gallery in London in 1939. "The charm of his style," Stephen said, "is the simplicity of his industrial landscapes. They draw us in but we remain outsiders, surveying the noise and bustle of the streets, but never able to participate." His work reflected his life. Lowry was a loner, friendly yet without close companions. He spent much of the 1930s struggling to look after his much-loved and bed ridden mother after his father's death, while also working as a rent collector. His art emerged during the night hours when he worked tirelessly in his studio, creating his landscapes populated with his famous so-called matchstick men and matchstick cats and dogs.

L S Lowry 1887–1976

Laurence Stephen Lowry was born in Stretford in March 1887, moving to Pendlebury in 1909 when the family fell on hard times. He drifted into office work with a firm of accountants in 1904, but later became a rent collector for a property company where he remained until 1952, despite the fact that his paintings began to sell after an exhibition of his work in 1939. He studied in the evenings at Salford School of Art between 1915 and 1928, giving up only when the demands of working as well as looking after his mother became too great. In 1967 the then GPO (General Post Office) chose Lowry's *Coming Out Of School*, which was painted in 1927, as a stamp while at the same time a major retrospective exhibition of his work toured the country. In 1976, just after he died, nearly 200,000 people visited the Lowry exhibition held at the Royal Academy.

Mickey Mouse tinplate barrel organ

Found in Morpeth, 1999. Valued at £6–10,000 (c.$11–18,000).

Small wonder that the owner of this delightful little clockwork tinplate barrel organ looked so pleased when expert Jon Baddeley told him its value. Until then, he had simply thought of it as a well-loved childhood toy, given to him around his fifth birthday.

"It has been well used, hasn't it?", remarked Jon as he examined it. "One of Mickey's arms is missing and Minnie is looking decidedly exhausted after all those years of dancing on top of the organ, but very early Disney toys are highly collected and any serious American buyer would be willing to overlook the damage."

Mickey Mouse

Invented by Walt Disney in 1928, Mickey was destined to become an overnight sensation and the subject of one of the most successful licensing operations of all time. Disney had lost the rights to his first cartoon character, Oswald the Lucky Rabbit and was determined to retain tight control on all subsequent creations.

Tinplate Mickey and Minnie Mouse

Found in Moreton-in-Marsh, 1997. Sold at Christie's in 1997 for £51,000 (c.$93,500).

Tipp & Co.

This German toy company was founded in 1912. By the 1920s it was making a wide range of good-quality tinplate toys at a time when Germany led the field in toymaking.

It was towards the end of a long, busy day in Moreton-in-Marsh in 1997 when Hilary Kay was presented with this very rare Tipp & Co. Mickey Mouse on a motorcycle. The toy was produced c.1929 and carried the manufacturer's trademark: a "T" intersected by a "C." It had been passed to the owner by his uncle who had been given it on his ninth birthday in 1930, a gift bought from Woolworths.

Not only was it in excellent condition, but Hilary identified it as one of only ten examples of the rare five-fingered Mickey motorcyclists that are still in existence. The toy is typical of early Mickeys, with a longer nose than those found after 1935, a toothy grin and what are called "piecrust" eyes – circular eyes with a triangular slice removed.

To add to the thrill, it emerged from its original box with a lithographed label. It is now thought to be the only example with the box intact. The presence of the box alone might have accounted for as much as £25,000 (c.$45,800) of the price that it realized at auction.

E H Shepard drawing

Found at Wills Memorial Building, Bristol, 1998. Valued at £10–15,000 (c.$18,000–27,500).

There are few names in the world of children's book illustration more guaranteed to revive happy childhood memories than that of E H Shepard. So Rupert Maas was delighted when an early Shepard drawing was laid before him at a Roadshow in Bristol. The owner had become friendly with Shepard's daughter many years earlier. Over tea one afternoon, the pair began talking about Winnie-the-Pooh and A A Milne's association with Shepard's father. The owner was invited to look through some of the artist's sketchbooks and fell in love with this drawing.

The drawing seems to indicate that Pooh was still the germ of an idea going through Shepard's head – he is so much slimmer than the bear we all cherish from childhood memory and his nose is much longer. Not only that, but Tigger doesn't appear until the later books; here he has sprung to life, fully formed. It shows a very interesting stage in the development of the artist's ideas.

Shepard's daughter offered the drawing as a gift with a little note confirming its authenticity. The owner insisted on paying something for it and a price of £10 (c.$18) was agreed. In commercial terms, the deal was an astoundingly good one for the owner, since Shepard's original drawings now sell for staggering sums.

Ernest H Shepard 1879–1976

Shepard and Milne's London birthplaces were within five minutes walk of each other, a prophetic circumstance given the iconic status they later achieved as creators of Winnie-the-Pooh. Shepard's maternal grandfather was a watercolour artist and his grandson began drawing at an early age, later winning a scholarship to the Royal Academy Schools where he met and married his first wife, Florence Chaplin. He enlisted in the army at the start of World War One and rose to the rank of major. He was also awarded the Military Cross for bravery. During the war, he sent jokes about battles to *Punch* and after 1914 joined the magazine, contributing a weekly drawing. It was through *Punch* that he met A A Milne and their collaboration began. *Winnie-the-Pooh* was published in 1926. Curiously, the drawings of Pooh were not based on Christopher Robin's bear but on Growler, the much-loved bear belonging to Shepard's son.

Silver-mounted claret jug

Found in Dorking, 1998. Valued at £20–25,000 (c.$37–45,800) for insurance.

Victorian silversmiths were famously skilled at producing novelty items, the best of which are now sought after by an international band of collectors. Animal cruet sets, pepper pots, pin cushions, menu holders and vesta cases often appear on the market, but Ian Pickford was astonished to see this rare claret jug arrive at the Roadshow.

Safely stored

The owners inherited it and, having had it valued many years ago at £950 (c.$1,700) for insurance purposes, kept it wrapped in newspaper in a trunk. They were persuaded to take it to the Roadshow by close friends with the happy surname of Duckworth, whose holiday home, Duck Haven, is filled with duck-related memorabilia. Get it valued, they said, and we'll pay you whatever it's worth.

They had a change of heart when their friends revealed the jug's astonishingly high value. It was made in 1881 by top silversmith Alexander Crichton, one of the best exponents of novelty claret jugs that were made over a relatively short period in Victorian London – this piece is a rare survivor.

"So many silver-mounted claret jugs get smashed. It would be quite impossible to replace the glass because it's specifically modelled as the duck's body with very fine engraving simulating the feathers," explained Ian. "The combination of the reputation of Crichton as a maker and the popularity of duck objects make this exceptionally desirable."

Alexander Crichton (1763–1856)

By 1880 Crichton had formed a partnership with another silversmith, John Curry. They traded as Crichton & Curry from premises at 45 Rathbone Place, Oxford Street, London, listed as "designers, modellers and silversmiths." They were known not only for this duck jug but for their other claret jugs modelled as owls, walruses, parrots, penguins and cockatoos. Even animal claret jugs such as crocodiles, carp and dodos, listed under other retailers, are thought to have been designed by Crichton. The partnership was dissolved in 1884 and by 1886 Crichton had declared bankruptcy, hit hard by a recession in the 1880s that affected the luxury market.

Lyre-shaped diamond brooch

Found at Worcester Cathedral, 1999. Valued at £4–£6,000 (c.$7,500–11,000).

Diamonds

Alexander the Great reputedly brought the first diamonds to Europe in 327 BC after his invasion of India. This hardest and most brilliant of stones was mined in India and then in Brazil until, in the mid-nineteenth century, a young child in South Africa was found playing with what turned out to be handfuls of diamonds. Today the majority of diamonds used in jewellery come from South Africa. Legend has it that diamonds quicken love between boy and girl and restore affection between man and wife.

If music be the food of love and of sorrow, then jewellery designers have long capitalized on the potency of musical symbols incorporated into brooches and pendants with a strong sentimental theme.

Geoffrey Munn was quick to notice the stunning quality of this lyre-shaped brooch, handed down to the owner through several generations of her family. The loop at the top allows it to be worn as a pendant and, typically for this type of jewellery, there is a hinged compartment at the back designed to hold a lock of hair. In the centre sits a somewhat pensive cupid painted in enamels, a powerful symbol of love.

Sentimental jewellery became highly fashionable during the Georgian period in England, with light, delicate styles imported from France following the Rococo style from 1730. This piece was made almost 100 years later (c.1810) and is set with lovely old diamonds, probably from Brazil, which glitter in a much more subdued way than the brilliant-cut diamonds of South Africa.

Floral diamond brooch

Dorking, 1998. Valued at £3,000 (c.$5,500) at auction.

Flowers and diamonds are a winning combination, which was why the owner of this stunning nineteenth-century brooch had a smile on her face even before she listened to John Benjamin's opinion. She inherited it from her mother's great-aunt, but the brooch scarcely saw the light of day; it had been stored away for four generations.

The central flower was mounted on a spring or *en tremblant,* so that it trembled enticingly as the wearer moved. The original fitted box had survived, a feature that adds interest and sometimes value to jewellery. What the owner hadn't realized was that concealed beneath the plush velvet in the box was a specially made long hairpin which allowed the brooch to be secured to the hair.

"The effect of this wonderful floral spray dancing around in the candlelight must have ensured that your ancestor's dance card was full before the evening had scarcely begun!", said John.

"Pins like this often accompany nineteenth-century brooches but few owners know where to look for them. I'm delighted to see that your brooch has survived in such complete condition."

Floral jewellery

Flowers were employed to great effect in Victorian jewellery when diamonds from South Africa became plentiful. Various species were modelled to convey messages of love: roses for happiness, pansies signifying that the loved one was constantly in the thoughts of the admirer, and the humble ivy for friendship.

Burdett scrimshaw carving knife and fork

Found at Scarborough, 2003. Valued at £10–15,000 (c.$18,000–27,500) and sold in San Francisco for $61,625 (c.£33,000).

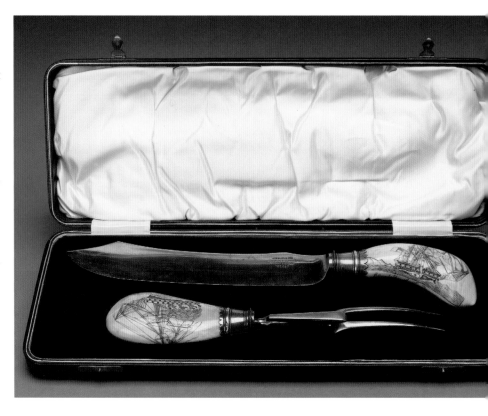

Hilary Kay says that it is always a delightful surprise to come across a genuine example of scrimshaw, in this case by Edward Burdett, one of the most important scrimshaw artists of the nineteenth century who lived and died by whaling.

Born in Nantucket in 1805, he became First Officer of the whaler *Montano of Nantucket* and died at the early age of 27 when, in close pursuit of a harpooned whale, he became entangled in the line and was dragged overboard to his death.

"I saw his hand in the carving as soon as I began examining the set," said Hilary. "He has a distinctive style and was one of the very first-known scrimshaw artists working in America. I spent time researching after the Roadshow and it turned out that the owners had lent the set to a museum for an exhibition and I contacted the curator who confirmed my findings."

Seafaring history

The family who brought this exceptional knife and fork to the Roadshow had owned them since the 1820s. The handles are the teeth of sperm whales engraved with whaling ships: the fork handle shows a burning ship, the *Daniel IV*, and the knife handle the *Elizabeth of London*. The men on board the latter rescued the crew of the *Daniel IV* in 1828 when, full to the brim with whale oil, it burst into flames. Previously, the *Daniel IV* earned a dubious reputation when it anchored in a Hawaiian port in 1825. Its crew, angered by the prohibition of women on board, roamed the streets threatening the inhabitants.

Hilary knew that the true value of the set would be realized in the United States and decided to quote a cautious auction value of £10–15,000 (c.$18,000–27,500). Once the owners had decided to sell in the States, a CITES (Convention on International Trade In Endangered Species) was applied for and granted, together with a Declaration of Antiquity. On the day the set came under the hammer at Bonhams and Butterfield, there was standing room only in the saleroom.

Scrimshaw

Although whales' teeth and bones were the main materials for scrimshaw, woods, metals and shells, as well as the ivory of animals such as the walrus and elephant, were also carved with nautical motifs. In order to qualify as scrimshaw, pieces must have a proper nautical association. They must have been carved by a sailor or involve materials from sea life. Sailors made their own tools to do the work and produced a huge variety of objects to give as presents, such as walking sticks, powder horns, chess sets, lace bobbins, spoons and rolling pins.

Jacobean high chair

Found at Llangollen, 1995. Valued at £3,000 (c.$5,500).

The owner of this very early and interesting high chair inherited it from his grandfather. Christopher Payne has previously come across children's furniture which has survived since the early seventeenth century, but not in this condition.

"It was so unusual to see one of these oak high chairs with the footboard still intact. Normally they're missing and you just see the evidence of where they've been, such as a series of holes for adjusting its height or a step in the frame that would have supported the footboard.

"We would also assume that there should be a bar across the arms to prevent the child falling out, but that didn't become a feature of high chairs until much later. It seems that most children were secured by a sash or belt around the waist or by the chair being pushed firmly under the surface of the table. As time went on, wealthier families had sets of dining chairs made with a high chair made to match."

Early children's furniture

This chair was made c.1620 when children were treated as small adults. Few concessions were made to their immaturity, and the concept of learning through play was undreamt of. Furniture made specifically for children was therefore confined to small versions of adult armchairs, small tables, high chairs and cradles. A few carved wooden dolls and other simple toys survive. Needless to say, only well-off families took the trouble to order furniture specifically to cater for the needs of their offspring.

Irish marquetry table

Found at Peebles, 1995. Valued at £4,000 (c.$7,500) for insurance.

The owner thought that his grandfather would have bought this Irish breakfast table to furnish his house of 1864. John Bly explained that it would have been a judicious second-hand buy around this date because it would have been brand new c.1850–60. Collectors appreciate the thick hand-cut veneers in yew, a wood highly favoured by Irish cabinetmakers, and the vibrant marquetry showing motifs that include a harp and Prince of Wales feathers.

Sadly, the centre of the table has suffered water damage. The stain is now part of the table's history, John said, and should be left alone.

Breakfast tables

Circular and oval breakfast tables were introduced at the beginning of the nineteenth century. Large tables for eight to ten people are rare and command high prices.

Made in two parts with the surface fixed to the pedestal base, they are vulnerable to alteration, often resulting in mismatched tops and bases that have been "married."

Richard Dadd painting

Found in Barnstaple, 1986. Bought by the British Museum in 1987 for £100,000 (c.$184,000).

Peter Nahum noticed a large painting packed between two pieces of cardboard as he walked to his table at the start of the Barnstaple Roadshow. Two hours later he was unwrapping one of the most historically important finds in the entire history of the *Antiques Roadshow*, a lost painting by Victorian artist Richard Dadd.

The painting was unsigned, but Peter was familiar with Dadd's work. The owners had thought it was a print; it had been hanging on the sitting-room wall and was about to be consigned to the garden shed while they redecorated.

Peter later consulted Patricia Allderidge, archivist and curator at the Bethlem Royal Hospital Museum in London, once an asylum. Dadd had been incarcerated there after being certified insane in 1844.

Patricia was able to match the painting with catalogue notes describing it as portraying travellers camping on the shores of the Dead Sea, painted c.1845.

Friends of Dadd at the time commented on the wonderful work he was producing, with bizarre inscriptions in mingled French and English on the back. This painting carried just such an inscription. Dadd had also written to friends describing the experience of camping by the Dead Sea while crossing the desert to visit a monastery.

A number of other lost Dadds have since come to light, and since it's likely that he gave away a substantial amount of work while at Broadmoor, there may be more waiting to be discovered.

Richard Dadd (1817–86)

Born in 1817 in Chatham, Kent, Dadd went to the King's School, Rochester and began drawing at the age of 13, using the River Medway, the Royal Naval Dockyard and the surrounding Kent landscape as inspiration. He began studying at the Royal Academy Schools in 1837, when he started to use subjects drawn from history and literature. In 1841, two of his small fairy paintings attracted great attention. In 1842 he was commissioned to tour Europe and the Middle East with Sir Thomas Philips, former mayor of Newport, and he now began to exhibit the first signs of the madness that was to blight his life. On returning to England, he murdered his father and was committed, first to Bethlem Hospital in London and then to Broadmoor, where he continued to paint, clinging to his identity as an artist. He died of consumption in January 1886.

George Richmond miniature

Found in St Helier, 1995. Sold at Bonhams in 1996 for £63,250 (c.$116,000).

When this highly important miniature ivory, just 21.6 x 14.6cm (8½ x 5¾in), arrived at the 1996 Roadshow held on Jersey, Peter Nahum gave it the highest value relative to surface area of anything he had ever seen at a Roadshow.

The artist was George Richmond and the miniature had remained with the family, coming down through Richmond's daughter-in-law. It went on the market in the nineteenth century, but fortunately was bought back by the artist's daughter Julia at a studio sale in Richmond-on-Thames in 1897 for £210 (c.$385).

"It came from the most intensely visionary and romantic period in British art," Peter maintained. "Entitled *In The First Garden*, Richmond painted it in 1828 at the age of 19 when he was living with a group of fellow artists and followers of the famed poet and artist William Blake in Shoreham, Kent."

The romantic idealism and simple way of life that Richmond followed at Shoreham with his wife Julia Tatham, whom he married in 1831, produced the lyrical serenity found in his art. However, it did not provide the regular income needed to support a large family. The couple had 15 children, ten of whom survived their infancy. Richmond then turned to portrait painting and became one of its leading exponents. His portrait of Charlotte Brontë hangs today in the National Portrait Gallery.

"I wish my husband were still alive to share this with us," said the owner when Peter revealed the astonishing value of this exceptional family heirloom.

George Richmond (1809–96)

Born in 1809, Richmond studied at the Royal Academy Schools, forming a lifelong friendship with Samuel Palmer. With Edward Calvert, they formed a small group based in Shoreham, Kent, called "The Ancients," who venerated the poet and artist William Blake. Their simple, pastoral life was based on the notion that ancient man was greatly superior to modern man. Richmond died in 1896, having exhibited at the Royal Academy over six decades.

Embroidered casket

Found in Cheltenham, 1995. Valued at £15–25,000 (c.$27,500–45,800) and current value £28,500 (c.$52,600).

Victoria Leatham, as curator of the collection at Burghley House in Stamford, Lincolnshire, is very well acquainted with this type of embroidered casket. The owner had inherited the casket ten years earlier, when it had been valued at approximately £3,000 (c.$5,500), but otherwise knew very little about it.

It represented a very good example of late-seventeenth-century embroidery and was produced during the reign of Charles II; the needlework carried out at this time by women at home in the wealthy households of England is considered to be some of the finest in existence. These embroidered caskets still come to light and always fetch many thousands of pounds at auction – particularly when they have survived in good condition through the years, as this one had done.

"When new, the colours would have been quite brilliant and garish, the sort of thing we would actually consider rather vulgar today," said Victoria. The wooden carcass of the casket is covered with panels of embroidery, which would have been separately worked in silk threads before being attached to the piece and then banded with silver thread. The lady of the household would have asked the estate carpenter to make up the chest, complete with drawers and a domed cover; the latter was designed to lift up, revealing a well for storing small objects.

"Pieces like this served as portable desks as well as jewellery boxes and vanity cases," Victoria added. Sometimes caskets of this type also incorporate secret compartments, accessed by pressing hidden buttons, and ladies could use them to hide love-letters in the process of being written, or those sent to them by admirers.

Stuart embroidery

The Stuart period encompassed the reigns of seven monarchs, from James I, who acceded in 1603, to Queen Anne, who died in 1714, with the drab Commonwealth sandwiched between Charles I and Charles II. Needlework became decidedly more opulent with the Restoration of the monarchy in 1660, the period when this casket was made. The mistresses of well-to-do households organized the gentlewomen and children under their authority in various projects to enhance the comfort of draughty rooms, including making samplers, bed hangings, coverlets and cushions. The best materials – gold and silver wire threads, silks, ribbons and laces in glorious colours – were bought from merchants. These were transformed into the animals, insects, flowers and figures that feature in work of this period, inspired by the well-tended gardens around the house and by Bible stories.

Burmantofts vase

Found at Harrogate, 2001. Valued at £6–8,000 (c.$11,000–14,700) and current value £12,000 (c.$22,000).

This magnificent and large twin-handled vase was made by Burmantofts of Leeds in 1899. It was brought in by the son of the general manager of the pottery, who remembered it standing in his father's office when he used to visit the factory. Henry Sandon, devoted as he is to the history of ceramics and their production, asked if he had had the chance to see the potters at work; he regretted he hadn't. In those days, Henry explained, it was rare for outsiders, especially youngsters, to be allowed to enter the inner sanctums of potteries, not just because of the dangers but because the craftsmen hated to be seen at work in case their secrets were revealed to the world.

New discovery

Since Henry looked at this pot, research has been carried out into the mysterious monogram, a form of the letters "L" and "K" on the base, and the artist has now been identified as Louis Kramer. This is an exciting development, because he "… was in a league far above other decorators at Burmantofts," said Henry's son, John Sandon. "The decoration in greens and blues, with strange fish swimming through weeds and fronds on the glazed faience (tin-glazed pottery) body, closely resembled the type of decoration used by William de Morgan which was based on early Persian pottery," Henry went on. "This style was hugely popular at the time. Around the top was a band of pseudo-Arabic script. The style had resonance with the Aesthetic Movement, which was just losing favour as Art Nouveau began to take hold."

Henry went on to explain that under the base of the vase was an interesting reference, "design 41," suggesting that it was an experimental piece, or possibly intended for showing at exhibitions. It is certainly unlikely that it was meant for sale. The owner remembered other large pieces standing in his father's office, presumably to impress visitors.

"Ordinary pieces of Burmantofts do not yet fetch high prices, but a pot of this quality is very special," said Henry. "It's at the top of the collecting tree, especially in the Islamic market."

Burmantofts

Burmantofts of Leeds made art pottery between 1882 and 1904 as part of the Leeds Fireclay Company. The company began in the 1850s as Messrs Wilcox & Co., manufacturing salt-glazed pipes, firebacks and other architectural ceramics in an area where both clay and coal were in abundant supply. After 1904, the Leeds Fireclay Company continued making utilitarian wares under the name Lefico and Granitofts, including toilets for places such as the Queen's Hotel in Leeds.

Mrs Ambrose's punch pot

Found in Liverpool, 1988. Valued at £5–6,000 (c.$9–11,000) and sold for £14,300 (c.$26,300).

Little did Mrs Ambrose know how drastically her life was about to change as she stood in the Roadshow queue at Liverpool in 1988. Secreted in a bag was the now-famous piece that her mother had always used as the family teapot and which Mrs Ambrose kept wrapped in a tea towel on top of the wardrobe. The pot was cracked and chipped and Mrs Ambrose was worried that, because of the damage, she wouldn't be allowed into the hall.

She turned out to be one of the great stars of the Roadshow. Her "teapot," in reality a mid-eighteenth-century Whieldon-type punch pot, was a very important find. David Battie delighted in revealing its value in steadily increasing amounts as the cameras rolled. "I asked her what she'd think if I told her it might be worth £150 [c.$275], building up until we got to £2,000 [c.$3,500] and finally quoting £5–6,000 [c.$9–11,000]. She was aghast! It was the perfect combination of delightful owner and wonderful object!"

Up for sale

The punch pot was entered for auction at Sotheby's with a reserve price of £5,000 (c.$9,000) and sold for £14,300 (c.$26,300). Mrs Ambrose then found herself in a position to buy the council house she had lived in for many years, and became a regular visitor to the Roadshow whenever it came to the north of England.

Whieldon-type wares

Made in creamware with the spout modelled as a snake and decorated with mottled green, yellow and aubergine-lead glazes, this punch pot belongs to a range of pottery known as Whieldon-type wares. Thomas Whieldon (1719–95), Josiah Wedgwood's partner (1754–9), was one of the century's most important Staffordshire potters and the first to develop mottled glazes which also include tortoiseshell and agateware. The powder colours were dusted onto the pieces before firing, mingling to create the unique effect. Many other small potteries produced similar wares, so unless they can be proved to have been made by Whieldon these pieces are referred to as Whieldon-type.

Shelley tea and coffee service

Found in Lowestoft, 1999. Valued at £2,000 (c.$3,500).

A rt Deco tableware is often brought to the Roadshow, but experts rarely see tea and coffee services in such perfect condition as this Shelley example in the vibrant "Blocks" pattern.

The service was an early version, launched in 1931, in the Vogue shape with solid triangular handles on the tea cups. "The cups were highly impractical because the handles were so difficult to grasp," Paul Atterbury told the owner. "Style triumphed over commercial considerations for a while," Paul went on, "but so few sold that the style had to change, making this set all the more desirable."

Shelley pottery

Shelley started life as Wileman & Co. in the late nineteenth century and then changed its name to Foley Potteries alongside the Foley China Works and then to Shelley in 1925. Eric Slater, who took over from his father as art director of Shelley's, was responsible for many of the strong and innovative designs and shapes manufactured by the company during the 1920s and 30s.

The Merry Man delft plates

Found at Keswick, 1999. Valued at £20–25,000 (c.$37,000–45,800).

H enry Sandon will never forget the lady at Keswick who, when asked what she had in her biscuit tin, replied "assorted biscuits" and then proceeded to unpack a full set of six Lambeth Merry Man delft plates.

"These are incredibly rare!", exclaimed Henry who regaled her with some of the figures realized at auction for the plates, finally revealing that this set could easily fetch in excess of £20,000 (c.$37,000).

The owner inherited them from her aunt, Dorothy, and remembered playing as a child with her cousin in front of the glass cabinet in which they were displayed. Together they would chant the famous inscriptions,

"What is a merryman
Let him do what he can
To entertain his guests
With many merry jests
But if his wife do frown
All merriment goes down."

Lambeth delft

It was during the seventeenth century that the production of delft (tin-glazed) pottery had spread from the east of London to both Southwark and Lambeth on the south bank of the Thames. Full sets of inscribed, dated plates like this are rare survivors.

Marklin tinplate biplane

Found at Chatsworth, 1996. Valued at £100,000 (c.$184,000).

Hilary Kay first set eyes on this rare Marklin tinplate biplane in 1987 while putting together an exhibition at Sotheby's for the Save The Children Fund. She visited Chatsworth House in Derbyshire, and although the Duchess of Devonshire didn't think she had anything to lend, she invited Hilary to look around. "I found the biplane on an open shelf in one of the rooms open to the public! We used it in the exhibition and when it was returned suggested it was moved to a safer home. When I returned to Chatsworth for a Roadshow in 1997, the biplane had been locked away in the gold vaults!"

Hilary filmed the biplane for the Roadshow, mentioning that the only other one known belonged to a Thai prince. After the show the programme received a letter from a lady who had been a housekeeper at the Duke of Devonshire's school. The duke and the prince had apparently been the best of friends.

The connection was fascinating. It meant that the pair had probably gone through the sumptuous Marklin catalogue before Christmas 1909 and both picked out the biplane as the present they most wanted. Luckily for them, their wishes came true.

It would have been an expensive toy, even at the time, produced by one of the most celebrated German toy manufacturers. Made of tinplate with 43-cm (17-in) diameter celluloid wings and a celluloid propeller, it was modelled on the Wright brothers' biplane of the period. Astonishingly – because Celluloid, which was an early form of plastic, is a highly volatile and brittle material – it has survived in marvellous condition.

Marklin

Tinplate was the most widely used material for toymaking during the nineteenth century. Marklin, established in 1859, became one of the best known of the German manufacturers, along with Bing and Carette and many of their models were accessible only to the very wealthy. Marklin was based in Goppingen and they produced mainly for export. Their trains were painted in liveries to match those of the country where they would be sold, and its ships also had the names and inscriptions changed according to the country. A huge range of rolling stock, stations, figures and accessories were available. German toymakers were badly hit by both world wars, but Marklin has survived to this day. Its boats, trains, cars and aeroplanes are sought after worldwide by collectors who appreciate the high quality maintained by producing a limited range of toys with great attention to detail.

Waterloo chest

Found at Poole, 1998. Valued at £25,000 (c.$45,800).

Roy Butler recognized the significance of this splendid chest as soon as he saw it. "I'd heard about Waterloo chests and I'd seen photographs of three of them, but I'd never actually had the privilege of handling one until the owner brought this in to the Roadshow. It was a great day for me!"

The owner rescued it from her father who had owned it for years but never liked it. He was about to consign it to the coalshed when she swooped in and rescued it. She took it to a restorer and, as her interest deepened, began to research its history.

Battleground tree

It's called a Waterloo chest because it's made from the trunk of an elm tree that was cut down on the field of the Battle of Waterloo. Apparently, the Duke of Wellington waited under the shade of this tree while his soldiers were forming up to go in to battle in 1815. Long after the historic victory, visitors began flocking to the area from far and wide, just to look at and touch the famous elm tree that had given shelter to the beloved hero of the battle.

The poor Belgian farmer who owned the field began to complain, and with very good reason. The tree had begun to die, probably because large portions of its bark had been stripped as souvenirs. An enterprising Englishman called John Children bought the entire trunk of the suffering elm in 1818. From the tree was made a throne for King George IV as well as several chests, including this lovely example.

All the wooden chests seem to be in this style, with small carved laurel-leaf wreaths applied to the centre of each door and a splendid lion mounted on the top, representing the Lion Mound at Waterloo in Belgium. "Waterloo" is also always inscribed around the base of the lion mount.

The Battle of Waterloo

The battle was fought 13 km (8 miles) south of Brussels between the French, under Napoleon Bonaparte, and the Allied army (a coalition of British, Dutch, Belgian and German soldiers) under the Duke of Wellington. Napoleon's final defeat in 1815 saw the end of 23 years of war between Britain and France and ended his dominance in Europe. Arthur Wellesley, the first Duke of Wellington, was one of Britain's most famous soldiers and statesmen who made his name winning battles in India, was knighted in 1805 and became Duke of Wellington in 1814.

Painting of an English country house

Found at Clacton-on-Sea, 1999. Valued at £20–30,000 (c.$37,000–55,700).

The family who owned this delightful painting of a grand English country house lived in "old" Harwich, once the dwelling place of wealthy merchants who built grand, comfortable houses and lived in a thriving community close to the busy port.

The owners had decided to uncover the original Tudor part of their house, which had undergone various "improvements" over the centuries including both Georgian and Victorian additions. As they removed a Victorian fireplace in one room, they soon hit what felt like stone. Thinking that it was probably the original sixteenth-century fireplace, they then realized that it was blocked off by a piece of board.

Astonishing discovery

Gentle probing revealed a solid wooden panel. They began to carefully remove layers of old wallpaper and saw evidence of paint. More careful soaking and they revealed this interesting early seventeenth-century painting of a grand English country house. Expert Peter Nahum was very excited by what he said was the most complete British house picture of the period he had ever seen. He particularly loved the way the painter had depicted the landscape around the house in an almost abstract, architectural style.

Itinerant artists

The style of this painting is very typical of house portraits done by Dutch artists for wealthy merchants in Holland, who commissioned paintings of their property in the seventeenth century as a way of displaying their wealth. The proximity of Harwich to the Hook of Holland meant that a number of these itinerant artists, who travelled around the country working to order, came to England to ply their talents among the equivalent class of English businessmen. English artists of the time had a similar system of working, producing so-called "primitive" depictions of houses, horses and carriages for farmers and merchants. Farmers also commissioned splendid portraits of their prize cattle. The aristocracy, on the other hand, commissioned artistic work from the famous leading painters of the day.

Majolica comports

Found at Worcester Cathedral, 1999. Sold for over £87,000 (c.$161,300).

It was only by chance that the owner of these valuable Victorian majolica comports became a visitor to the Roadshow. She and her husband wanted to try out their new senior citizen passes on the local railway and took the first train they saw from their home near Birmingham. It was going to Worcester, and once there they saw the banners and posters advertising the forthcoming Roadshow at the cathedral.

They returned on the specified day with what the owner referred to as "one of mother's cake stands" in a rucksack. David Battie immediately recognized her inherited piece as a George Jones majolica comport. On hearing that she had four more, David sent her home to collect them. "I was rather afraid she wouldn't come back!" said David.

Allegorical subjects

The five comports were not quite a complete set, since there would originally have been six. In a grand Victorian house with a large formal dining room, they would have been piled with fruit and placed at regular intervals along the length of the table during the dessert course. Three of the surviving comports represented the continents, a buffalo for North America, a camel for Asia and a lion for Africa. Originally, there would also have been a piece representing Europe. Of the other two, one featured a fox and the other a hound.

David was astonished to come across one owner with so many good pieces of George Jones majolica. "They were wonderful things; I think George Jones was better at majolica than Minton. Americans clamour to buy this stuff and they ended up doing extremely well at auction. The buffalo comport made £29,250 [c.$54,000], the lion £26,950 [c.$50,000], the camel £16,600 [c.$30,800] and the fox and hound sold as a pair for £14,875 [c.$27,600]."

English majolica

The term refers to the earthenware covered in thick, brightly coloured lead glazes that was produced in England from the mid-nineteenth century. It was developed by Leon Arnoux at Minton's who was inspired by the pottery of a much earlier time, particularly Italian maiolica. Other factories soon took it up, including Wedgwood and George Jones.

Punch mustard pot

Found at Haywards Heath, 2001. Valued at £15,000 (c.$27,500) for insurance.

The magazine of humour and satire called *Punch* was first published on 7 July 1841 and ceased publication in 2002. It struggled in its early days, but enjoyed enormous success and a high circulation once it had captured the imagination and affection of the British people. It inspired any number of small novelty silver items at a time when novelty silver was hugely popular. Perhaps the most common are the small stamped-out silver ashtrays representing the front cover of the magazine.

"Until the Roadshow at Haywards Heath, I had never seen a Mr Punch mustard pot," said expert Ian Harris. "Owls often appear in sets as a mustard with two smaller birds as the salt and pepper, so it is probable that this magnificent Punch would originally have been accompanied by Judy and Toby the dog as a complete set. In fact, I've seen Toby dog peppers on their own, but this pot is extremely rare, which is why I gave it such a high insurance value."

The figure of Punch

Mr Punch is the most enduring rascal in the history of puppetry, a marionette in medieval times who changed into a glove puppet in the nineteenth century. His exact origins are unclear, but the figure today has direct links with the *commedia dell'arte* figures of the seventeenth century. His wife, originally named Joan, appeared in the eighteenth century and they have bickered their way down the years, eventually joined by the dog, the baby, the policeman, and the crocodile.

Set of four French silver candlesticks

Found at Henley, 1995. Valued at £20,000 (c.$37,000) for the four.

Ian Pickford was astonished when he saw this set of four French candlesticks, made between 1730 and 1740 and inherited by the owner from her father. "Pre-Revolutionary French silver is very difficult to find," Ian explained. "So much of it was destroyed during the French Revolution, either looted or melted down for coinage. In fact, you're more likely to come across examples of it outside France because so much was made to commission by top French craftsmen and exported. Catherine the Great of Russia, for example, ordered vast quantities of French silver, and there are also good examples in Great Britain. These candlesticks were not by a top Parisian silversmith but by a very good maker working in provincial France, and made at a time when the aristocracy was allowed to own silver. Louis XIV (1638–1715) ordered the aristocracy to destroy its silver."

Ian would have been pleased to see a single candlestick of this quality and date, but to come across four was undreamt of. "It was extraordinary that four had remained together. They were beautifully cast and the octagonal bases made them particularly desirable. When you get sets like this, you don't simply double and quadruple the price of a single, you add on either a third or half as much again."

Cast candlesticks

This cast set was made by pouring the molten metal into a mould and then soldering the two halves together. Many candlesticks are made of thin sheet silver that is rolled out before the sections are soldered, resulting in a much lighter, and less desirable, gauge. These are usually filled with pitch in the base to give them weight.

Silver tankard

Found at Cannock Chase, 1998. Valued at £4–5,000 (c.$7,500–9,000).

Alastair Dickenson was delighted to come across this piece of Irish silver in the thoroughly English setting of Cannock Chase.

"Not only was it Irish, but it was made in Cork and this upped the ante considerably. As with Scottish silver, pieces made away from the main centre, in this case Dublin, are of enormous interest. Had it been made in Dublin, it would have been worth considerably less. Other important provincial towns in Ireland include Limerick, Youghal, Kinsale, Kildare and Galway, and pieces from these centres tend not to have a date letter, just a town mark and maker's mark."

William Clarke

The tankard carries the maker's mark of William Clarke, one of the more interesting silversmiths of Cork. In 1709–10 he was Warden of the Company of the Society of Goldsmiths of the City of Cork and he became Master in 1714. This tankard has no date letter but would have been made in the early eighteenth century.

Crawley silver

Found in Crawley, 1993. Valued at over £200,000 (c.$371,600). Part of the collection was subsequently sold at auction in 1994 for £78,000 (c.$145,000).

Every Roadshow expert begins the day hoping to see something exceptional, but Ian Pickford could hardly have predicted the treat that was in store for him at Crawley in West Sussex.

A young man and his mother arrived and began pulling piece after piece of fine English silver out of carrier bags. "It was the very best collection I have ever seen at a Roadshow," Ian said. "The pieces kept coming until I eventually valued the total haul at over £200,000 [c.$371,600]."

The owner's late husband had developed a genuine passion for silver and had accumulated this impressive collection throughout the 1960s and 1970s. His widow had no idea of the full extent of the collection until she began to find pieces that had been carefully packed away in different parts of the house, together with the all-important receipts.

Objects included tankards, amongst them a rare Commonwealth example of 1653, a rare three-compartment snuff box of 1740, a stag's head stirrup cup and a box inlaid with a piece of the famous Boscobel oak in which the exiled future Charles II sheltered.

Wine bowl

This is just one object from the Crawley silver collection, a James I wine bowl of 1607 that sold in 1994 for £13,000 (c.$24,000). It was later sold at Christie's for £28,750 (c.$53,400). It is believed to be the only James I silver example in existence.

Bohemian glass vase and cover

Found at Poole Arts Centre, 1998. Valued at £4,000 ($7,500).

Expert Michael Newman was astonished that this valuable mid-nineteenth-century Bohemian glass vase had survived in completely undamaged condition.

The owner had inherited it from his grandmother, and it was stored precariously balanced between piles of books awaiting his move from the family home to his own flat! He was a descendant of the Victorian painter Edward Ladell, but had a far greater interest in music than in fine art.

Michael described it as a *tour de force* of the art of wheel-engraving, with its meticulous facets around the base, stem, lower section of the bowl and the impressive spire knop. The facets were then highlighted by outlining them in amber, the same colour used on the bowl, which was wheel-engraved with a scene of deer in a forest.

Bohemian glass

The country now known as Czechoslovakia has a long and fine tradition of glassmaking. Bohemian glassmakers of the mid-nineteenth century prided themselves on the skill of wheel engraving. Landscapes including animals were a favourite subject, as were battles, horses and hunting scenes. On this example, a layer of amber glass was laid over the clear body and then engraved to reveal the stag and trees in the clear glass. The second layer provided a good surface for cutting and engraving.

Japanese cloisonné vase

Found at Winchester College, 1999. Valued at £3–4,000 (c.$5,500–7,500).

The owners arrived at Winchester for the Roadshow with this exceptional cloisonné enamel vase that was wrapped only in a flimsy plastic bag – it was an heirloom inherited from an aunt over 20 years previously.

"You must take very great care of it from now on!", admonished David Battie. "Cloisonné is virtually impossible to mend when it gets damaged and this is a really lovely vase, made c.1890. The wisteria design is so unusual because it's been created using gold and silver wire rather than brass."

Cloisonné enamel

The first stage of creating cloisonné enamel is to cover the base metal body of the piece with a network of wires or cells (the French word for cell being *cloison*). This network is then filled with fine coloured enamels that have been ground down to make a paste – it is the metal strips that keep the colours apart. The piece is then fired and polished.

Powell & Lealand microscope

Found in Stoke-on-Trent, 1993; valued at £21,000 (c.$39,000). Current value up to £25,000 (c.$45,800).

This microscope, manufactured in 1842 by Powell & Lealand, was an exceptional find for Hilary Kay and represented the pinnacle of nineteenth-century scientific-instrument making.

The owner's great-great-uncle paid 30 shillings (the equivalent of £1.50 today) for the microscope. He also received a huge range of fascinating accessories, including an insect holder; this, along with the fact that the original lacquer on the gleaming brass was intact, added considerably to the value.

A similar microscope sold in 1992 for a world record of £25,000 (c.$45,800). While this one's auction value was £21,000 (c.$39,000), the owner was advised to insure it for £35–40,000 (c.$65–74,000).

Powell & Lealand

Hugh Powell and Peter Lealand started their company in 1842. Nearly all of their microscopes showed the date of manufacture and the company's address. The business ceased trading in 1914.

London delft portrait dish

Found at Mansion House, 2002. Valued at £8–12,000 (c.$14,700–22,000).

It was appropriate that a man who worked on building sites in the City of London should bring with him the broken pieces of a rare mid-seventeenth-century London delft dish to a Roadshow held in the City.

Over many years, he had collected pieces of pottery that had become revealed as sites were excavated, but he struck gold when he found this dish. It made David Battie's day.

The naively painted portrait in the centre is of the Duke of York. "Happily, he made the wise decision not to try to stick the dish back together," said David. "I have never seen another one like it and I doubt I shall again."

English delft

Delft is tin-glazed earthenware. It probably started to be produced in England around the mid-sixteenth century when Flemish potters settled in East Anglia. By the end of the century, several workers had moved to London, specifically to Aldgate in the City, and then to other parts of the country including Bristol and Liverpool.

Beilby armorial wine glass

Found at Metrodome Centre, Barnsley, 1997. Valued at £6–10,000 (c.$11–18,000).

The combination of the magical name of Beilby and the armorial decoration on this eighteenth-century wine glass made it one of the most exciting finds of John Sandon's career on the Roadshow.

John is highly knowledgeable on the work of the Beilbys, who bought the glass pieces and decorated them. "The Beilbys … discovered a way of enamelling on glass where the temperature was so highly controlled that the decoration was fused onto the surface without melting the wine glass itself." He goes on to say that "Their pieces painted in white enamel are desirable enough, but armorial glasses in coloured enamels are extremely rare. This wine glass … is sitting in an ugly wooden base because half the foot is missing."

Prized possessions

"These pieces were always precious, so if one got damaged a way was found to preserve it. If it had been complete, I would have put a value of £30–40,000 [c.$55,500–74,000] on it. A good Beilby bearing the royal coat-of-arms would be worth £75,000 [c.$139,000], whereas other large ones sell for between £40–50,000 [c.$74–92,000]."

John explains that, "The double series opaque-twist stem is absolutely typical of the Rococo period and was in high fashion when this piece was made c.1765. The decoration shows a fancy cartouche and insignia with the 'C' shapes and asymmetrical scrolls, again typical of the period."

Beilby glass

Enamelling on glass became more widespread in Britain after 1760, and the Beilby family was one of its main exponents. William, the fourth of seven children, was apprenticed to a maker of enamel pieces (snuffboxes and so on) in Bilston in the West Midlands, one of the main centres of this work in the eighteenth century. After his father's business failed, the family moved to Newcastle, where William established a successful business painting with enamels on clear glass, a technique that he had begun to use earlier. His sister Mary joined him and their work soon became widely admired. William painted in both white and coloured enamels, but examples of the latter are much rarer. Flowers, fruiting vines, hops and barley were favourite subjects, as were detailed scenes of classical ruins, landscapes and sporting events.

Early Kakiemon vase

Found in Cheltenham, 1995. Valued at £9–12,000 (c.$16,500–22,000).

The owner of this exceptional Japanese Kakiemon vase always suspected that it was something out of the ordinary, but was teased mercilessly by her family, who scoffed at its slightly crude-looking decoration of Japanese buildings in a landscape executed in blue, green, dark red and a very significant shade of yellow.

The vase came into her life when her husband's grandparents died and each of the grandchildren was invited to choose something from the house. There were many other grander things on display, but she was attracted by its shape and colour.

Landmark development

"Your instincts were right," Victoria Leatham told her, "Your vase is a very early example of Japanese Kakiemon porcelain made in Arita c.1660–70. It was around this date that these potters first discovered how to use yellow in the range of colours included in their palette, so this piece is very important historically, as well as being a beautiful object. The murkiness of the yellow is an important clue to the date it was made."

Kakiemon porcelain

Made in the Arita area and exported from the port of Imari, Kakiemon wares are named after the legendary Sakaida Kakiemon, who allegedly developed a style of enamelling on porcelain in the mid-seventeenth century. In appearance, this vase is not typical of standard Kakiemon wares, which have a restrained, sophisticated style of mainly floral decoration against a milky white body covered in a colourless glaze. The overglaze enamels include dark red, blue, turquoise, a pale manganese, a murky yellow and black. Kakiemon wares mainly include small dishes, bottles, vases and bowls, but a few rare models of human and animal subjects were also produced.

Carpathia memorabilia

Found in Poole, 1998. Valued at £50,000 (c.$92,000).

The sinking of the *Titanic*

The "unsinkable" *Titanic*, the pride of the White Star Line, sank on her maiden voyage on 15 April 1912. The captain was said to be determined to break all records for an Atlantic crossing and was ploughing at great speed towards New York, ignoring warnings of icebergs. The tragedy has held a morbid fascination for many ever since, and *Titanic*-linked memorabilia now changes hands for enormous sums.

This extraordinary collection of rare memorabilia relating to the ocean liner *Carpathia* was inherited by the owner from her father, Dr Edward McGee, an Australian who trained as a doctor in Scotland and became the medical officer on the *Carpathia*.

The collection consisted of a photograph of Dr McGee, a gold *Carpathia* medal given for bravery, a medal from the Royal Humane Society and a cigarette case inscribed "Presented to the Captain, officers and crew in recognition of heroic services."

"The Carpathia went to the rescue of survivors of the *Titanic*," Victoria Leatham explained. "The value of memorabilia relating to the tragedy has rocketed in recent years. The last time a gold *Carpathia* medal came up for sale in 1997 it made U.S.$30,000 [c.£16,300]." The Royal Humane Society medal is also of enormous interest to anyone who collects memorabilia relating to the *Titanic* disaster.

Boxwood okimono

Found at Lyme Park, Cheshire, 1998. Valued at £2–3,000 (c.$3,700–5,500).

The breathtaking detail on this enchanting little boxwood okimono, just 4cm (1½in) high, told David Battie that it could only have been produced by one of the top Japanese family of carvers working in the mid-nineteenth century.

The owner found it in a chest of drawers he bought for £35 (c.$64). The modelling is so realistic that he thought he'd come across a pair of fossilized dead frogs. He had no idea which Roadshow specialist might be qualified to talk about fossils, but he took it along anyway and was delighted to discover its real origins and its value.

Japanese okimono

An okimono is a carved ornament, usually in ivory, but also in bone and boxwood. They were made in great numbers by Japanese craftsmen for export to the West from the mid-nineteenth century. Japanese men had by then ceased to wear traditional costume.

Craftsmen who had spent their working lives fashioning the netsuke (toggles) and inro (compartmented boxes) which men wore hanging from their waists had to make other objects such as this. Happily, Western buyers clamoured to buy them.

Gold pocket watch

Found at Michelham Priory, 1996. Valued at £25,000 (c.$45,800).

The original receipt for this extremely rare English gold pocket watch proved that it was bought in 1920 from the Sheffield Goldsmiths' Company for £77 8s. 6d. (£77.46), then a considerable sum.

It has a *tourbillon* (the French for whirlpool) mechanism that rectifies the timekeeping errors caused by the wearer's movements. The escapement revolves continually, a highly complicated mechanism to produce, and it was entirely hand-made. This rare watch was made to order for the original owner.

Top English watchmakers

The high value of this watch lies in its technical superiority, as well as the rarity of the *tourbillon* movement. Only a few companies operating at the time would have been capable of producing a watch of this fine quality. They included Frodsham, Bent, S Smith & Son, Nicole Nielsen, and Victor Kullberg, mostly small firms in London. Each employed highly skilled craftsmen.

Kreussen tankard

Found at Worcester Cathedral, 1999. Valued at £6–8,000 (c.$11,000–14,700).

The squat shape and typical decoration on this German tankard were immediately recognizable to Gordon Lang – the owner had recently inherited it from her mother but knew little about it.

"These dumpy looking humpen (tankards or mugs) in brown stoneware, decorated with brightly coloured enamels, were produced in Kreussen near Bayreuth in Bavaria mainly in the seventeenth century. Your piece is absolutely typical, with this wide-moulded band in the centre featuring the Apostles and inscribed with a religious text, 'Remember me and this gift from God.'" This was a particularly rare example from the period most sought-after by collectors.

German stoneware

This distinctive, high-fired pottery was produced in great quantities and to very high standards at various centres in Germany during the sixteenth century, particularly in the Rhineland, Saxony and Bavaria. *Apostelhumpen* is the term for vessels decorated with the Apostles. Other themes are the planets and hunting scenes.

Lloyd's Patriotic Fund sword

Found in Ipswich, 1985. Valued at £8–9,000 (c.$14,700–16,500).

After a fairly quiet day Roy Butler took a short break from his table, and as he walked across the room, he saw the lion's head of this sword protruding from a carrier bag being carried by a gentleman coming towards him. The late recording made the perfect end to Roy's day.

A fitting reward

Swords like this were given as honorary awards by the Lloyd's Patriotic Fund to officers who had served at the Battle of Trafalgar. The Committee met on 3 December 1805 and decided that swords to the value of £100 (c.$180) each – a considerable sum then – should be presented to surviving captains and to commanders of His Majesty's ships who had been involved in the action.

In addition, swords worth £50 (c.$90), of which this is an example, and some worth £30 (c.$55) were awarded to certain other officers. Elaborately decorated, each was inscribed for the recipient and intended to be worn only with full dress at official functions, or if the recipient was sitting for his portrait. They look impressive, but would have been flimsy and clumsy as fighting weapons.

Officers were given the option of choosing a silver vase by Rundell, Bridge & Rundell rather than the swords and some preferred the former, which could be displayed as a trophy. The vases that belonged to Captain Edward Rotheram, flag-captain of the *Royal Sovereign* and Captain Capel of the frigate *Phoebe* are now in the splendid Nelson Collection at Lloyd's in the City of London. The collection also includes one of these honorary swords.

Lloyd's Patriotic Fund

The Lloyd's Patriotic Fund is the oldest British fund of its kind in existence today, inaugurated at a meeting held on 20 July 1803 at Lloyd's coffee house in the Royal Exchange in London. Two months earlier, war between Britain and France had broken out again and patriotic fervour was at its height. The Fund's committee had few problems entreating companies and individuals to contribute to its noble cause. Donations poured in, and by March 1804, £179,000 (c.$330,000) had been received. The committee granted sums of money to those wounded in action, as well as bestowing annuities on the dependants of those who were killed. A further use of the fund was to give rewards in the form of money, or swords such as the one shown here, to those who had fought so heroically against the French.

Young woman in profile

Found at Coalville, 1998. Valued at £15–20,000 (c.$27,500–37,000).

The pensive tranquillity in the pose and the expression of this young girl caught Peter Nahum's eye as the owner unwrapped the painting at a Roadshow in the East Midlands.

"This is a really wonderful example of the work of Thomas Benjamin Kennington, a portrait and genre painter who was born in Grimsby and is known for his paintings of mothers and children. If you look carefully you can see he has signed only with his initials, 'T' and 'K', but I know for certain this is his work."

Thomas Benjamin Kennington 1856–1916

Pathos and emotion are the hallmarks of Kennington's work. He studied at the Liverpool School of Art, the Royal College of Art and the Académie Julian in Paris. He was one of the founders of the Imperial Arts League, and exhibited at the Royal Academy between 1880 and 1916 and at the RBA and the Grosvenor Gallery.

Garden idyll

Found at Greenwich, 1998. Valued at £5–6,000 (c.$9–11,000).

The owner of this charming Victorian painting was in for a pleasant surprise when she took it to the Roadshow. It had belonged to the lady who lived at the end of her street. "She hated it and kept it behind the sofa, eventually giving it to my mother," she told Mark Poltimore, who roared with laughter. "It was painted in 1859, very much in the Victorian chocolate-box tradition, by a very well-regarded artist called Charles James Lewis, known for his figures and landscapes. Paintings like this are highly commercial, so I fear your neighbour might well regret her decision if she knew how much it was worth!"

Victorian genre painting

Artists in the mid- to late-nineteenth century excelled at capturing life in rural England, depicting country people, their cottages and surroundings in an idealized manner to satisfy rich city clients who wanted to believe in the existence of a romantic, rural idyll. In reality, country life was one of extreme poverty.

Franz Bergman owl diptych

Found at Syon Park, 1998. Valued at £800 (c.$1,450).

The clear maker's mark "NAMGREB" on the base of this intriguing cold-painted bronze owl told Eric Knowles that it was produced by Franz Bergman, a sculptor at the turn of the century who tended to use his name spelt backwards on his more risqué models. Erotica of any kind is always highly sought after. The "secret" contents of this wise old bird account for at least £500 (c.$900) of its value. This is typically the type of "nod, nod, wink, wink" object that was passed round with the port by groups of Victorian gentlemen after the ladies had retired to the drawing room.

Franz Bergman

Bergman was a sculptor working in Vienna around the turn of the twentieth century, producing a wide range of highly collectable cold-painted bronze animals and figure groups, such as Arab carpet sellers and other North African traders, in a huge range of sizes.

Lowestoft cat

Found at Houghton Hall, Norfolk, 2001. Valued at £5,000 (c.$9,000).

The owner of this rare and valuable little Lowestoft cat noticed it nestling at the bottom of a box of junky ceramics on display at a local auction house and bought the lot for £2 (c.$3). She subsequently took it to Norwich Museum as well as to various dealers to try to establish its history. No one felt confident enough to confirm its authenticity until she took it to the Roadshow, where Chris Spencer, a Lowestoft specialist, assured her it was genuine and probably one of only six surviving Lowestoft cats that were made around 1780.

Lowestoft animal models

Lowestoft is best known for its blue-and-white wares, but also produced a series of animals including pug dogs, cats and sheep. Two of these cats are in the Norwich Museum and three in private hands. This may well be the last survivor to be found.

Carved wooden doll

Found in Ashford, 1993. Valued at £10–15,000 (c.$18,000–27,500).

It is rare for good-quality English eighteenth-century carved wooden dolls to appear on the Roadshow, which was why Bunny Campione was so delighted to see this example. Unusually for such pieces, it had come down through the male line of a family.

Wooden dolls were also made in Germany during this period, but this is typically English, with dotted eyebrows and lashes, fork fingers and square, crudely pinned hips. The tip of her nose is slightly chipped, but otherwise she's in excellent condition, unusual for a doll of this age. Her original striped silk-taffeta dress, stiffened corset and little slippers have also survived.

Carved wooden dolls

Late-seventeenth-century dolls have painted eyes, whereas by the start of the eighteenth century, enamel, pupil-less eyes, like the ones on this doll, have begun to appear. By the end of the eighteenth century, fingers are shorter and more primitive looking, necks slimmer with a more pronounced slope to the shoulders and waists have disappeared. Nineteenth-century dolls have more crudely painted faces and less shapely legs.

Mid-eighteenth-century silk-brocade shoes

Found at Windermere, 1995. Valued at £4–5,000 (c.$7,500–9,000).

A wealthy mid-eighteenth-century noblewoman would have had these shoes made to match an opulent open robe, ordered for a special occasion such as a wedding or grand event at court. They have survived in remarkable, condition complete with the pattens made to be worn outside in the streets. The owner thought they must have belonged to her great-great-grandmother because the soles are marked "Petty," her mother's maiden name.

Mid-eighteenth-century shoes

The slightly rounded toes on this pair are a change from the very pointed shoes that were in vogue earlier in the century. The fronts would probably have been covered with a buckle. Early on buckles were small, but gradually they became more ostentatious.

Meissen tea service

Found at the Children's Roadshow, Basingstoke, 2001. Valued at up to £20,000 (c.$37,000).

Lars Tharp was astonished when this beautifully decorated Meissen tea service of c.1735 arrived at a Children's Roadshow. The owner was a 14-year-old schoolgirl who had inherited it from her grandmother. Although manufactured by Meissen, it was an outside-decorated or *Hausmalerei* service, consisting of the coffee pot shown here and a variety of other pieces. The palette was easily identifiable, including an egg-yolk yellow and a slightly mucky green which the Meissen factory rarely used until it was improved. The insects are large and eccentric-looking, unlike the much smaller ones that are seen on factory-decorated Meissen of this period.

Outside-decorated porcelain

Hausmalerei is the German term used to describe porcelain that leaves the factory undecorated or "in the white" and is then decorated elsewhere. Further research revealed that the work on this service was probably carried out by the daughter of Johann Auffenwerth, who ran a decorating studio in Augsburg.

Art Deco figure group

Found at Reading, 1999. Valued at £2,500–3,000 (c. $4,500–5,500).

At 74cm (29in) long and 36cm (14in) high, this large silvered bronze figure group makes an impressive and stylish statement. The owner bought it in 1998 in New York for $3,000 (c.£1,600)– about the right price, thought Eric Knowles.

It was signed Z Covat, not a name that Eric has encountered in his many years of specializing in Art Nouveau and Art Deco objects. "This is a wonderfully elegant and very typical piece of its day on a stepped marble base, but nothing like as valuable as it would be if it were by one of the leading sculptors of the 1920s and 30s."

The scene is of Diana the huntress pursuing deer. The theme is very typical of the period. The solitary figure of Diana symbolizes the emancipation of women during this period when they were enjoying new-found freedom after the end of the First World War, and the sense of speed she conveys was another very important feature of Art Deco, a period when records were being broken on land, sea and air.

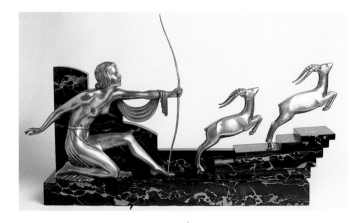

Art Deco sculpture

Sheer style gives this piece considerable value, but a well-known signature will always send prices soaring. Top names of the period include Marcel Bouraine, Joseph Lorenzl, C J R Colinet, Ferdinand Preiss and Dmitri Chiparus.

Silver-mounted coco-de-mer bowl

Found at Lyme Park, Cheshire, 1998. Valued at £3–4,000 (c.$5,500–7,500).

Jim Collingridge has examined a variety of valuable early silver-mounted coconut cups, but was entranced when a visitor to the Roadshow brought along this fascinating seventeenth-century vessel, a gift from an aunt who had no place for it in her home.

It was made from coco-de-mer, the double coconut native to the Seychelles Islands. The fruits take ten years to ripen and the nut-like portion under the fleshy, fibrous casing is generally two-lobed. "These nuts were found floating in the Indian Ocean and were regarded with the kind of fascination we find difficult to understand today," Jim explained.

"Nuts like this were treated as precious objects. The smooth shells were hollowed out and engraved and then embellished with lavish silver mounts. Much of the work was carried out in Europe, but I think yours was done in India."

"Natural" vessels

The bounty of mysterious and exotic lands was treated with enormous reverence in the seventeenth century. Coconuts, cowrie shells, elephant and rhinoceros tusks, ostrich eggs and even the humble gourd were transformed into precious objects – standing cups, ladles and, later, snuff boxes and nutmeg graters.

Mughal gold bracelets

Found in Peebles, 1995. Valued at £10–15,000 (c.$18,000–27,500).

These brilliantly enamelled and jewel-encrusted mid-nineteenth-century Indian bracelets are known as *kadas*, and were handed down by the owner's great-grandmother who was given them by a Mughal prince. Each is formed as a confronting serpent studded with table-cut diamonds and lashing ruby tongues. Such pieces normally formed part of a bride's dowry, worn around the ankle or upper arm.

The Mughal dynasty

The Mughal dynasty ran from 1526 until the death of Emperor Bahadur Shah in 1858. Jewellery acted as a statement of the wealth and influence of its rulers. Many workshops produced a fabulous legacy of precious necklaces, hairpieces and bracelets.

Album of Japanese prints

Found at Greenwich Royal Naval College, 1998. Valued at £2,500–3,500 (c.$4,500–6,500).

Japanese works of art have remained a firm favourite for David Battie throughout his career, so he was thrilled to come across this pristine selection of nineteenth-century Japanese wood-block prints by Toyokuni at Greenwich, bought by the owner's husband from a junk shop in 1947. "They had survived in unusually good, fresh condition because they were bound in an album and had thus been protected from fading. Prints like this often came to the West as wrapping paper around ceramics and other works of art. They were passed around amongst artists, particularly the Impressionists, and had a huge influence on their work."

Toyokuni (1769–1825)

This artist was one of the masters of the Japanese woodblock print, known for his realistic depictions of Kabuki actors. Toyokuni belonged to the Utagawa School of artists, elevating it to a position of great respect and power in the nineteenth century. The prints in this album were probably created by his son-in-law, Toyoshige.

Children playing in the sea

Found at Glamis Castle, Angus, 2000. Valued at £10–15,000 (c.$18,000–27,500).

This delightful painting was brought in by the owner's daughter-in-law, casually wrapped in a black dustbin liner. The owner had bought it for a very reasonable price at an auction in Dundee in the 1970s and it had hung on the landing wall ever since.

Rupert Maas explained that it was painted by Robert Gemmell Hutchison in the closing years of the nineteenth century, when he was trying to escape the cloying sentimentality of the previous generation of Victorian painters. "You can see the naturalism in this work and the beautiful quality of light he has introduced. The paint in some of his later pictures looks caked, but this is in very good condition."

Robert Gemmell Hutchison (1860–1936)

The artist Robert Gemmell Hutchison enjoys an enormous following, especially in his native Scotland. He was a landscape, figure and portrait painter and studied in his early years at the Board of Manufacturers' School of Art in Edinburgh.

Ferdinand Preiss figure

Found in Bexhill-on-Sea, 1994. Valued at £8,000 (c.$14,700) and current value the same.

A specialist in Art Nouveau and Art Deco, Eric Knowles was delighted to come across this impressive example of the work of the German Art Deco sculptor Ferdinand Preiss. Using the expensive combination of ivory and bronze known as "chryselephantine", it displayed superb carving.

"There are so many fakes on the market today, made of resin in the Far East, that it was a pleasure to come across one that was so obviously genuine and in such good condition," said Eric. "The fakes have very badly finished bases with artificially rusted nuts and rods securing the figures to them. They also have dirt rubbed into the crevices and are usually of patinated metal rather than bronze." The condition of the figure was also a pleasant surprise: "The ball she is holding is made of celluloid, a very brittle and vulnerable material, so it is remarkable that it survived intact."

The piece, made between 1930 and 1936, was unusual for two further reasons. First, the base was inscribed "Ada May Lighter Than Air", and second, the embossed and gilt paper label put on before the piece left the foundry had survived. Ada May was a famous actress and dancer of the period. She obviously made a great impression on the artist, for, although Preiss did model actresses, he is more widely known for his sporting figures playing golf or skiing.

"Ada was standing on quite an elaborate stepped base – architectural in form and composed of different coloured marbles – which added slightly to her value. Plain bases of Brazilian green onyx, for instance, are slightly less desirable," said Eric, "but the value really lay in the quality of the figure."

Ferdinand Preiss (1882–1943)

Ferdinand Preiss's desirable Art Deco figures "... don't have the theatrical qualities of figures produced by other artists, such as Colinet or Chiparus," said Eric. "He went in for these eerily life-like creatures, very Aryan and athletic, with anatomically correct facial features and limbs." The ivory face was given a dainty wash of paint to make it even more realistic. His work was manufactured at the Preiss-Kassler Foundry in Berlin, established in 1906. Ceasing production during the First World War, Preiss resumed in 1919 and by 1929 employed several designers. His work has been much copied, often using a softer stone and with over-elaborate bases, so "Preiss figures" should be treated with caution.

Steiff teddy bear

Found at Burghley House, 1997. Valued at £2–3,000 (c.$3,500–5,500).

Collectors set great store by each bear's expression, and this one has a particularly appealing and slightly wistful look. Bunny Campione explains, "He was made by Steiff, which always helps value," she said, "but he has another interesting characteristic. He's called a 'centre-seam bear' because there is a seam running down through his snout. He was made with the end of one bolt of cloth and the beginning of another. Only every seventh bear got this treatment, so they're rarer and very sought after. "He was well loved, however, and collectors prefer their bears to be in good condition. In perfect order, he'd be worth £4–6,000 (c.$7,500–11,000).

Steiff bears

Steiff is best known for the bears that were made after Margarete Steiff's nephew, Richard, joined the company. These were modelled realistically, based on sketches he drew of bears at Stuttgart Zoo. Today, Steiff bears in good condition reach six-figure sums.

Steiff skittles

Found in Gainsborough, 1998. Valued at £8–10,000 (c.$14,700–18,000) for the set.

This pristine set of Steiff skittles or ninepins had sat in the attic for almost 100 years before they were brought to the Roadshow by their owner, who was celebrating her 91st birthday.

Jon Baddeley was astonished by their almost-new condition. "The reason they have survived without the knocks and dents I'd expect to see on a set like this is that there isn't a ball to throw at them. They've obviously hardly been played with at all."

The only person who handled them over their long incarceration was the owner's daughter, who was allowed to play with them for an hour or two when she was unwell. On the side of each little animal figure was the all-important little button, the signature of maker Margarete Steiff.

And why is the figure on the left taller than the rest and wearing a luxurious red jacket and crown and wielding a rather menacing-looking baton? Why, because he's the King Pin, of course!

Steiff toys

As a child Margarete Steiff was crippled with polio, so she began making dolls and animals from felt remnants. She was soon in charge of a thriving business – one that continues to this day. Steiff is most famous for its bears, but a wide range of dolls and other animals were also produced. Margarete Steiff died in 1909.

William Burges silver-mounted bottle

Found in Skegness, 1996. Valued at £30,000 (c.$55,700) and current value up to £50,000 (c.$92,000).

William Burges (1827–81)

William Burges was a bizarre and eccentric figure, an architect and a designer working in the most elaborate Gothic Revival style, designing furniture, metalwork, jewellery and wallpapers. He was involved with the rebuilding and remodelling of the interiors of Cardiff Castle, in 1865, and Castell Coch, near Cardiff, ten years later, for his friend and client the Marquis of Bute. Burges's house at 9 Melbury Road, London, is a masterpiece, filled with colour and with ornate and intricately worked pieces.

The most exciting discoveries are often the most unexpected. Paul Atterbury had left the table for a few moments when someone from Reception tapped him on the shoulder and showed him a small, around 18cm (7in) high, silver-mounted bottle. It was a moment of magic. The piece had arrived around 4 p.m., just as the doors were about to be closed, carefully wrapped and nestling in a shopping basket.

By looking at the style of decoration and the signature on the mount, Paul knew at once that it was a rare piece designed by the eccentric nineteenth-century English designer and architect William Burges. Moreover, it had been lost for over a hundred years.

Paul hurried back into the hall to share the find with fellow enthusiast David Battie, and together they talked to the owner in front of the cameras, revealing its history while she filled them in on its whereabouts over the last 50 years. Her father had bought the piece in 1949 in a junk shop off the Great North Road. She had treasured it for sentimental reasons, not realizing just how important it was.

The bottle itself is eighteenth-century Chinese porcelain covered in a coffee glaze. The silver Burges-designed mounts are in the form of organic tendrils and trees encasing the body; a spider set with pearls sits on the cover. Burges's name and a date, 1864, are carried on an enamel band at the base. From the Tudor period onwards, elaborate mounts were added to pieces of porcelain (or even to coconuts and other objects considered rare and exotic).

By creating this piece, and many others of similar design, Burges, who worked in the Gothic Revival manner, was producing a treasury of pieces in his own inimitable version of this style. Burges made a number of these objects for his own pleasure, keeping them at his house in Melbury Road in Kensington, London. Much of his work, including this bottle, was photographed in the late nineteenth century, the album eventually finding its way into the Victoria and Albert Museum in London. By referring to the definitive book on Burges, Paul and David were able to match the photograph with the piece that stood in front of them.

In 1996, Paul and David valued it at £30,000 (c.$55.700), and in 1988 Sotheby's sold a jewelled and decorated Burges bottle for £40,000 (c.$74,000). Today, this example could be worth between £30,000 (c.$55,700) and £50,000 (c.$92,000).

Army gold medal

Found at Michelham Priory, 1996. Valued at £8,000 (c.$14,700) and current value £8,500 (c.$15,700).

Roy Butler felt almost humbled when he saw this large British Army gold medal. "I've seen these before," he said, "but I've never actually had the privilege of handling one. So few were awarded by the Government that they are extremely rare. They were given during the Peninsular War of 1808–14 and the war of 1812." The owner was a descendant of Major-General Frederick Maitland, who fought against the French at Martinique in 1809.

Some of the first of these medals were given to the 13 officers who had formed part of a small British force under Major-General Sir John Stuart, who defeated the French at the battle of Maida in Calabria, southern Italy. They were small gold medals, measuring 38mm (1½in) in diameter, with the head of George III on the obverse and inscribed "Georgius Tertius Rex." On the reverse was the figure of Britannia, casting a spear with her right hand and with the Union shield on her left arm.

By 1810 it had been decided to award medals of one size with the battle's name engraved (though that for Barossa was die-struck) on the reverse. Medals were struck to commemorate the battles of Roleia and Vimiera, the cavalry operations at Sahagun and Benevente, and the battles of Corunna and Talavera in Spain in 1808 and 1809.

This large medal is 54mm (2⅛in) in diameter. On the obverse is the figure of Britannia seated on a globe. She is wearing a helmet and holds a laurel wreath in her right hand and a palm branch in her left. Beside her is the head of the British lion and her left hand rests on a shield charged with the crosses of the Union. On the reverse is the name of the engagement – "Martinique." It hung from a ring and was worn around the neck suspended from a crimson ribbon with blue edges. The smaller medal was made to the same design, but was worn from the buttonhole. Production of both medals ceased in 1814.

Military medals

Although officers had been rewarded for their bravery, the first medal to be issued to every man who served, regardless of rank, was the silver Waterloo Medal of 1815. The war against France had rumbled on from 1793 until 1815, and those soldiers who had gone to Spain and Portugal to fight the French in the Peninsular War of 1808–14 felt very disgruntled about the recognition of their naval compatriots' bravery when they themselves returned home empty-handed. This continued until Queen Victoria decided, in 1848, to institute a General Service Medal (GSM) to every man who had fought in the Peninsular War. However, there were no posthumous awards – only survivors could receive a medal, and for every battle fought one bar across the ribbon was awarded. The GSMs with several bars across, showing that one man survived many encounters over several years, can be worth over £1,000 (c.$1,800), while a medal bearing only one bar for one of the more obscure battles may have a value of £6–700 (c.$1,100–1,300).

William Kent-style table

Found in Colchester, 1994. Valued at £15,000 (c.$27,500).

Extraordinarily, this elaborately carved side table was found by its owner in a junk shop in Hampshire over 50 years ago with a price tag of £60 (c.$110), a princely sum at the time. Unable to afford it then, he returned to the shop a year later and found it still for sale at the same price. Expert Deborah Lambert dated it to c.1730–40, explaining that it was made in the style of William Kent whose ideas and designs were so influential in this period. The detailed carved base is pine, which would once have been richly gilded, and the top is marble.

Although Kent's influence is obvious, the table was not made under his direction. "Look at the best Kent furniture somewhere like Houghton Hall in Norfolk," said Deborah, "and you will see that the sphinxes are perfectly proportioned, whereas these have huge heads, matronly busts and puny hindquarters. Whoever made this was inspired by ancient Rome, in particular by Nero's Golden House, which contained frescoes depicting combined human, plant and animal forms.

William Kent 1684–1748

One of the most important English protagonists of the Palladian style of architecture in the early eighteenth century, Kent was also a landscape gardener, an interior decorator and a furniture designer. His designs were often copied by leading cabinetmakers of the day.

Renaissance gold plaque

Found in Farnham, 1991. Valued at £30–50,000 (c.$55,700–92,000). Would be hugely expensive today.

Renaissance works of art

The Italian Renaissance began to flourish in the late fourteenth century. Powerful dynasties such as the Medici and Borghese families patronized great artists and craftsmen who created the sculpture, architecture, paintings and metalwork of the period.

Simon Bull is an authority on clocks, watches and scientific instruments, but also a connoisseur of Renaissance works of art. Fortunately, he was on the team when this rare and beautiful gold plaque, made between 1570 and 1580, was brought along to the Roadshow. The owner inherited it from her father who had been a collector.

Simon recognized its importance immediately. It was one of a group of six plaques reputed to have been mounted originally on an Italian cabinet owned by the Borghese family, one of the wealthiest and most powerful in Italian society at the time. Similar plaques are housed in a major museum in Berlin. Originally these were thought to be the work of Benvenuto Cellini, considered by many the greatest goldsmith of his age. However, further research now suggests they were made by another celebrated goldsmith of the period, De la Portas.

The four corners are set with cornelians, and the scene shows Atalanta and her fellow hunters killing the savage boar that laid waste the lands of King Oineus. This famous legend is often depicted in painting and works of art of the Renaissance.

Ambrosia by Robert Walker MacBeth

Found at Woking, 1997. Valued at £10–15,000 (c.$18,000–27,500).

Robert Walker MacBeth 1848–1910

A Scottish artist, born in Glasgow, his father was the well-known portrait painter Norman MacBeth (1821–88). Robert was a painter of genre and outdoor contemporary scenes, often depicting the countryside and the people who worked there, but he is best known as an illustrator, mainly for the *Graphic*. He came to London after studying at the RSA (Royal Scottish Academy) Schools and first exhibited at the Royal Academy in 1871. He became an ARA (Associate of the Royal Academy) in 1883 and a member in 1903.

The owners of this life-size painting measuring 180 x 150cm (71 x 59in) were veteran auction hounds. They became very discouraged at one auction at a country house sale in Surrey, however, when every item they were tempted to bid for realized a price well in excess of their budget. At the end of the sale, the auctioneer suddenly announced that he was offering several unsold lots from the previous day "without reserve," including this picture described as "English School, 1880". No one else seemed terribly interested and it was knocked down to them for £550 (c.$1,000).

Known artist

Expert Philip Hook was astonished that no one in charge of the sale recognized the work of Robert Walker MacBeth, especially as the painting is signed with his monogram. "It's such an energetic, happy painting showing a serving girl, obviously in a busy tavern, delivering trays of ale and oysters to her waiting customers."

MacBeth's work shows a variety of styles. Some of his more detailed paintings look almost Pre-Raphaelite, others are of a much more humble composition. This is very typical in that it shows a girl engaged in her everyday working life. He depicted both women and children at work very skilfully, but some critics feel that the faces in some of his compositions portray a blank expression and a lack of draughtsmanship. His better-known works include *At Liberty*; *A Lincolnshire Gang* (1877), *Potato Harvest in The Fens* (1878), *Sedge Cutters* (1878) and *Sheep Shearing In The Fens* (1889).

MacBeth is best known as a prolific illustrator for the *Graphic*, the weekly magazine founded in 1869 by William Luson Thomas. Thomas worked as an engraver in Paris and then at the *Illustrated London News*. He left to take the brave step of launching the *Graphic* and recruited an entire team of talented artists such as Luke Fildes, Hubert von Herkomer, Frank Holl and Robert Walker MacBeth, all of whom toiled in the engraving studio producing woodcuts, sketches and engravings of daily life and events in Great Britain. By 1882 the company owned three buildings and 20 printing machines, and employed 1,000 people. The artists, MacBeth included, learned to produce high-quality illustrations to very tight weekly deadlines.

Oil painting of terriers

Found in Dorking, 1998. Valued at £6,000 (c.$11,000).

Mark Poltimore was bowled over by this large 101.5 x 119.5-cm (40 x 47-in) picture of two terriers by W Walker Morris, an artist who exhibited between 1850 and 1867. "You can't fault it!" exclaimed Mark. "Everyone who has walked past it has stopped to admire it. Just look at how alert and lively these little terriers appear, eagerly awaiting their master's return."

The owner had failed to appreciate the painting, thinking of it simply as "those little dogs" that had hung in his parents' hallway.

Victorian sentiment

From the mid-nineteenth century the urban leisured classes began to commission paintings of their beloved cats and dogs, animals that in the previous century had been largely unappreciated as pets. There was no better exponent of this sentimental genre than W Walker Morris.

Painting of a red gum tree

Found in Leeds, 2002. Valued at £40–50,000 (c.$74–92,000) for insurance.

Sir Arthur Ernest Streeton is considered one of the leading Australian painters of the early twentieth century, so Philip Hook was both surprised and delighted when this large and magnificent Streeton depiction of a red gum tree appeared at a Roadshow in the north of England. The painting was brought to this country in 1948 and was later inherited by the current owner.

"Streeton painted this in the 1920s, after he returned from England to settle back in his native Australia," said Philip. "It's a rare treat for us to see a really good Australian painting in this country. What is always so distinctive about them is the way the light is depicted and Streeton has captured it wonderfully here," he said, pointing out the thick, bold streaks of light-coloured oil paint that bring the edges of the branches and the trunk of the tree to life.

Sir Arthur Ernest Streeton 1867–1943

Streeton studied at the National Gallery School in Melbourne. During the First World War he worked for England as a war artist but returned to Australia in 1919. He was knighted in 1937.

Carved-bone watch stand

Found in Jersey 1995. Valued at £2,500–4,000 (c.$4,500–7,500).

A crowd of experts gathered round when this delightfully quirky pocket watch stand was unveiled at the Roadshow. It was brought in by a visitor who bought it during the 1970s for only £10 (c.$18). It falls into the fascinating category of prisoner-of-war work, produced in great quantities by French soldiers incarcerated in England during the Napoleonic Wars.

These unfortunate men were kept in harsh conditions but, ever resourceful, salvaged and dried the ox bones from the kitchens of the prison camps and carved them to make a wide range of both useful and decorative objects which were sold in the street markets around the gates of the prisons. The money helped them buy extra rations and other goods which made life more bearable.

This exotic example is not remotely typical of the objects made by the prisoners. Experts agreed that it may have been created by a prisoner who came from one of the colonies in Africa or even further afield, or that it might even have been made to commission for a client who dictated the design.

French prisoner-of-war work

Detailed models of ships, chess sets, work boxes and caskets, bobbins and even minutely detailed buildings carved to scale are typical of the type of work produced by these men, who also used their straw bedding to weave exquisite mats and boxes. Apart from their decorative bone and straw work, they also did a good trade making and selling counterfeit coins, which flooded Portsmouth c.1810. After the end of the conflict in 1815, 24,000 French prisoners were repatriated.

Fused Japanese noodle bowls

Found at Torquay, 1999. Of highly speculative value.

When Lars Tharp first saw these extraordinary scraps of Japanese porcelain, he thought that two bowls must have suffered an accident in the kiln. Their owner, however, told him that they were relics of the American bombing of Hiroshima. Her husband, a naval officer, had acquired them when he visited Japan shortly after the Second World War. They were ordinary mid-twentieth-century noodle bowls fused together in the heat of the nuclear explosion.

"To begin with I felt very depressed by what seemed to be a miserable relic of an horrific event, but within seconds I realized that they were symbols of monumental importance, iconic fragments surviving from a moment in which the world changed forever. In a sense, they're priceless in the same way as the relics of saints are above value, although I think you have to place them in the same category as the memorabilia that survives from the sinking of the *Titanic* or other famous wrecks."

"What was also significant," Lars went on, "is that the material, being porcelain, survived that incredible heat, when so much else was totally destroyed."

The Hiroshima bomb

On 6 August 1945 at 09.15 and 15 seconds precisely the Japanese city of Hiroshima was destroyed by the first atomic bomb, dropped from the aircraft *Enola Gay*. 140,000 people died. On 9 August another atomic bomb was dropped on Nagasaki and on 14 August the Japanese surrendered to the Allies.

Tiffany-style lamp

Found at Witney, 2001. Valued at £20–30,000 (c.$37,000–55,700).

Visually striking and beautifully made in bronze and stained glass, this 58.5-cm (23-in) high lamp looked for all the world like a Tiffany piece, but it wasn't marked.

"It looked like many of the products of the Tiffany studio of c.1910, and the quality was of the same high standard," said expert Paul Atterbury, "but because it wasn't marked I had to assess it as a good lamp of the same period and style but by another unknown maker. For that reason, I gave it a lower value than a Tiffany lamp carrying an embossed mark on the bronze section, a metal plaque on the shade inscribed 'Tiffany Studios, New York' and a reference number on the inner rim – this would have been worth in excess of £40,000 (c.$74,000)."

Tiffany design

"It was still a magnificent and very decorative piece," Paul went on. "It also said a great deal about the kind of influence Louis Comfort Tiffany had on the decorative arts at this period. He had many imitators. This was the time when electric light was transforming people's lives in the United States. His lamps were objects of great beauty but also highly functional and commercial. Tiffany had long years of experimentation with glass behind him when he began to produce and market his range of lamps after 1897. They were an immediate success, seen as sculptures in their own right with the brilliant shades made from glass left over from larger stained-glass projects. Designs were inspired by nature in the best Art Nouveau tradition, with dragonflies, peacocks and flowers in bloom featuring strongly."

Glass had been used over a long period to reflect candlelight, but electric light created a harsh glare. A Tiffany lamp softened the mood of any room, and he provided eager customers with a vast array of ceiling, floor and table lamps from which to choose, setting up an assembly line at the Corona works to put them together. Small wonder that other manufacturers were keen to get in on the act.

American glass

It was after the American War of Independence (1775–77) that American glass began to be produced in any quantity. Before this, most had been imported from England. Once British imports halted, skilled workers from other countries such as Ireland and Bohemia began to establish glassworks, producing glass in a variety of European styles. An innovative American technique was the development of mechanically produced pressed glass, resulting in affordable decorative glass flooding the market. At the end of the twentieth century, the production of coloured Art Nouveau glass was dominated by Tiffany, but among his imitators were firms such as Duffner & Kimberley, Frederic Carder at Steuben Glassworks and Martin Bach, who had worked for Tiffany and set up his Quezal Art Glass & Decorating Co. in 1901.

English globe bottle

Found at the University of Birmingham, 2000. Valued at £10–12,000 (c.$18,000–22,000).

Seal bottles

This is a typical shaft-and-globe-shaped bottle of a type that was made in England from the middle of the seventeenth century until c.1700 in a very dark green glass. There are no seams on these bottles because they were free blown. Typically, this one has a pronounced ring around the neck just below the rim which was used to tie a stopper onto the bottle. Many of these bottles are either dug up from the ground or found in water, which will have damaged the surface.

Henry Sandon is known for his excavating skills and has uncovered many early pots in and around Worcester, so he was able to tell the owners of this important seventeenth-century wine bottle that, judging by the pitting all over it, the bottle had evidently been buried for many years before it had come into their possession.

The owners had bought it in the 1950s from an antiques shop in Devon for the princely sum of £4.10 shillings, or £4.50 ($8) in today's money. Intrigued by the seal, they researched the coat-of-arms and discovered that it belonged to Sir Robert Hanson, who had the bottle made to celebrate his knighthood in c.1650. Later he became Lord Mayor of London.

"Bottles like these were used to serve wine that was kept in casks," Henry pointed out. "Often the seals identify an inn or the individual owner. In this case, the early date combined with an important owner made the bottle very valuable."

Gustave Vichy automaton

Found at Bognor Regis, 1980. Valued at £3–5,000 (c.$5,500–9,000) and sold in 1996 for £84,000 (c.$155,700).

This very rare late-nineteenth-century Gustave Vichy bird-trainer automaton was one of the great finds in the early days of the Roadshow. Hilary Kay was only 23 at the time, and by her own admission still learning. She had handled other automata but had never seen anything so fine, and knew instinctively that this was a unique piece.

The bird-trainer had always been known by his owner as "Charles." Her grandfather bought him as a present for his daughter in a house sale in Kent in 1897 for £3.10 shillings, in today's money £3.50 ($6). When he died in 1926, Charles was bought by the family for £7 ($13) and remained with them until he was sold in 1996.

When activated, Charles brings a flute up to his mouth and plays with articulated fingers to the accompaniment of a cylinder musical movement. The bird then moves his head and beak and repeats the tune learned from the flautist. The only other known example in such wonderful condition is part of a famous collection held in New York.

Gustave Vichy (1839–1904)

Gustave Vichy was one of the most successful nineteenth-century French automaton makers. The son of mechanical toymakers Antoine and Geneviève Vichy, he was born in 1839 and began his working life in 1864 as a mechanic and clock maker in Paris, soon earning a formidable reputation for his automata. His wife Thérèse dressed his figures and, as the firm flourished, guided numerous other seamstresses. Gustave continued directing the company until his death in 1904.

Fabergé animals and brooch

Animals found on the Wirral, 1996. Valued at £6–8,000 (c.$11,000–14,700) each.
Brooch found at Chatsworth, 1996. Valued at £5,000 (c.$9,000).

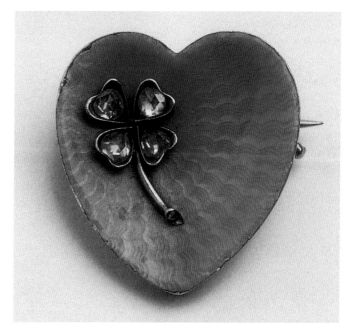

Geoffrey Munn was rather shocked when the owner of these Fabergé animals, each only 8cm (3in) long, revealed that her children had played with them. However, he was rather more composed than she was when she heard their value.

Her story would probably have made Carl Fabergé smile. He loved children and, much to his customers' surprise, would often settle their children on the floor to play with his carvings. The Royal Collection at Sandringham, Norfolk, contains 500 of these hardstone animals. Fabergé was commissioned by Edward VII to produce these carvings, in various coloured stones, depicting many of the animals found at the royal residence at Sandringham. The pig is carved from rhodonite and the elephant from rock crystal, the hardest and rarest form of quartz and very difficult to work. Most of the stones Fabergé used came from the Urals and Siberia; among these were chalcedony, agate, obsidian and nephrite, while for the eyes he used rose diamonds and cabochon rubies, and he sometimes modelled legs and tails in silver or gold.

Geoffrey often rummages through a family jewel box at the Roadshow. Far from risking missing the one good thing among the piles of baubles, he finds that anything of quality shouts out to him. The owner of the Fabergé heart-shaped enamelled brooch confessed that she was a jewellery addict. "She bought mainly at auction," said Geoffrey, "and never paid more than £150 (c.$275) for anything. The brooch was in a bag ... She paid £30 (c.$55) for the lot, and when I told her what it was and how much it was worth she gasped and burst into tears."

"It symbolizes luck in love," Geoffrey continued. "The diamond quatrefoil is for luck and the heart, of course, represents love. The four diamonds are worth only around £10 (c.$18) each. The value has nothing to do with the materials and everything to do with its being a wonderful piece of artistic jewellery from the workshops of Fabergé."

Carl Fabergé (1846–1920)

Carl Fabergé's family were Huguenots who fled France in 1685 and settled in St Petersburg. Carl's father was a goldsmith who gave him a thorough training in the family business. By the age of 24, Carl had taken control of the business. After delivering one of his bejewelled Easter eggs to Tsar Alexander III in 1884 he was granted the royal warrant. In 1900 he exhibited all the Imperial Eggs at the Exposition Internationale Universelle in Paris and was decorated with the Légion d'Honneur. When the Bolsheviks took over the house of Fabergé after the 1917 Revolution, he fled to Switzerland and died there in exile in 1920.

Irish peat buckets

Found at Whitchurch, 2001. Valued at £50,000 (c.$92,000) for the two.

This magnificent pair of peat buckets is uniquely Irish, so Christopher Payne was delighted to see them at an English Roadshow. He was also pleased to find that they had remained with the same family since they were made in the early nineteenth century.

Buyers love things that are fresh to the market rather than those that do the rounds of dealers and auction houses. "Irish antiques are highly sought after today, and because peat buckets weren't made in England, Scotland or Wales, they are both scarce and desirable. I love the way the strong ribbing swirls all the way down the length of the bucket rather than horizontally around them, which is more common. They're also big at 89cm (35in) high – other examples I've seen have been around 43cm (17in) high."

Natural source of fuel

The peat buckets would have sat on either side of a grand fireplace in a big country house to store peat, then the main source of fuel. With the depletion of woodlands in Ireland, the peat bogs were exploited both domestically and for industry. Rights to cut peat were allocated to landowners, and the turves that filled these buckets would have been stacked and cut by the servants of the household, who would have transferred them from humbler buckets into this handsome mahogany pair.

Both buckets were in bad condition. "Far better that than if they had been heavily restored," said Christopher. "They had been heavily used for nearly 200 years, so they were falling apart! One was held together with orange binder twine but that didn't matter. Work was needed to fix the brass bindings because they were coopered in the same way as barrels, but then all they needed was a bit of polish. The patina on both was fantastic! They really were a remarkable find!"

Irish furniture

There is always a strong demand for good Georgian Irish furniture from collectors in Ireland itself, as there is for Irish glass and silver of the same period. Craftsmanship thrived and amongst the top cabinetmakers in Dublin during the eighteenth and nineteenth centuries were Mack, Williams & Gibton, Gillingtons, James Hicks, Robert Strahan of Henry Street and Arthur Jones of St Stephen's Green. The hanging, carved centre shell, elongated acanthus shapes and triffid feet are all distinctly Irish characteristics found on furniture of this period.

Gillows marble-topped table

Found at Renishaw Hall, 2002. Valued at £30–40,000 (c.$55,700–74,000).

Orlando Rock was thoroughly impressed by every aspect of this rare Gillows table. The owner's mother bought it at auction in 1938 from the Barlborough Hall house sale of contents in Derbyshire. At the time, they were given to understand that it was one of only two made.

"What was so marvellous about this table," Orlando explained, "was not only the superb quality of the walnut and burr walnut frame, but that almost every single part of it was stamped with the name of the famous firm of Gillow of Lancaster. They were a fantastically important firm of cabinetmakers, established in the eighteenth century, who arguably reached the height of their commercial success during the Regency period in the early nineteenth century when this table was made. It's a sublime example of their work, a really fantastic piece of furniture."

Grand Tour piece

The surface of the table was composed of a jewel-like selection of different types of marble on a black marble ground. "These are incredibly rare marbles, ranging from porphryry and bianco e nero to Spanish brocatelle, verdi antiquo and even malachite," Orlando went on. "The malachite is particularly interesting from a dating point of view because it didn't start to appear in Italian specimen marble tabletops until the start of the nineteenth century. Around the edge were pieces in pebble-like formation with a chess board laid out in the centre. The quality of the work is really breathtaking."

The top would have been commissioned and brought back from the Grand Tour of Italy as a smart holiday souvenir, and given to Gillows to provide the base. Tables of this rarity and quality seldom appear on the market, which is why Orlando had no hesitation in giving it a high auction estimate.

Gillows

The Gillows firm was founded by joiner Robert Gillow in 1727 in Lancaster, which had a thriving shipbuilding industry. The firm imported mahogany and traded in rum and sugar. Furniture-making soon became Robert Gillow's main business. His eldest son, Richard, became his partner in 1757. In 1776 another son, Robert, opened and ran their showroom in London and managed the warehouse in the Oxford Street site where Waring and Gillow remained in business until the mid-1970s. Huge success followed the opening of the London showroom. The firm's output was vast. They undertook the refurbishment of entire buildings, fitting out the interiors and supplying all the furniture. Pieces made between c.1780 and 1817 are clearly stamped "Gillow Lancaster." All the order books and salesmen's archives survive, now housed in the library at Lancaster University.

Lewis Carroll collection

Found at Blenheim Palace, Oxfordshire, 1994 and Oxford, 1997. Valued at £150,000 (c.$278,500) including letter and photographs.

As if the thrill of seeing so many Lewis Carroll first editions at the Blenheim Roadshow were not enough, Clive Farahar had the pleasure of meeting the owner once again at Christ Church, Oxford, the author's own college, three years later. This time, letters and photographs had been added to the collection.

It was the sheer quantity and quality of the collection that was extraordinary," said Clive. "As a child, the owner's aunt knew Carroll. It is possible that she was one of his little girls. All the volumes were presentation copies, signed by the author in the lilac ink that he always used."

Translations included

The owner had copies of *Alice's Adventures in Wonderland* and *Through the Looking Glass and What Alice Found There* translated into French, Dutch and German. "He also had *The Hunting Of The Snark*, *Phantasmagoria* and *Sylvie and Bruno*," said Clive, "but Wonderland and Through the Looking Glass are the books that have really captured people's imaginations – and the most exciting aspect of the whole collection was that everything was in pristine condition. Not a dog-eared volume amongst them!

"I thought the collection might be worth £50–60,000 (c.$92,000–111,500), but once I had seen the letter written by Lewis Carroll to the owner's aunt, Annie Rogers, and the photos, I upped the value considerably."

The first 50 or so copies of *Alice's Adventures in Wonderland* were issued in July 1865, but the reproduction quality was poor; a second edition came out in November of the same year. The unbound pages of the first edition were shipped to the United States, given a new frontispiece, and issued in 1866. Alice was an immediate success, appearing in several languages. The sequel, *Through the Looking Glass and What Alice Found There* was published in 1871.

Lewis Carroll (1832–98)

Charles Lutwidge Dodgson was born in 1832, the son of the rector of Daresbury in Cheshire and the third of 11 children. Educated at Rugby, he arrived at Christ Church, Oxford in 1851 and graduated in 1855, when he was appointed sub-librarian of the college with which he was to be associated for the rest of his life. Although he earned his living as a lecturer in mathematics, he began writing poetry and prose in 1845, and in 1856 started to use the pseudonym Lewis Carroll. In July 1862, an entry in his diary reads: "I made an expedition up the river to Godstow with the three Liddells; we had tea on the bank there, and did not reach Christ College again till half past eight." This may be the first indication of the telling of *Alice's Adventures in Wonderland*, one of the most important books in the history of children's fiction. Lewis Carroll, as he is now remembered, died in 1898.

Pair of library globes

Found at Darlington, 1990. Valued at £30,000 (c.$55,700) the pair. Current value up to £65,000 (c.$120,700).

In the days when groups of wealthy gentlemen gathered at their clubs and in one another's homes to discuss the latest voyage of discovery or the newest development in science, a large pair of globes, one terrestrial and one celestial, on handsome stands was an essential piece of furniture for the library, no less important than a writing table and comfortable chairs. As the discussion went on late into the night, the globes slowly revolved. The terrestrial globe was consulted on matters relating to the earth and the journeys of the great explorers, while the celestial globe was studied on questions of the movement of the heavens. During daylight hours library globes were used for educational purposes by the children of the house, working with their tutor. If the household did not possess a pair, the tutor brought his pocket globe with him.

The owner of this elegant Regency pair brought the globes to the Roadshow at Darlington on behalf of his father-in-law. The latter had inherited them from his father, who had bought them 40 years earlier in a sale in the south of England. They were insured for £5,000 (c.$9,000), and it was a shocked son-in-law who prepared to return home and reveal their true worth. The maps are by Cary, one of a number of leading makers of globes in London at this time. Made in 1828, the paper maps were pasted over the original ones of 1816 – a common way of updating globes as voyages of discovery took place. Although in good condition, they needed some dry stripping to restore the original glorious colour. The globes still revolved well, an important feature for collectors. The stands resemble rosewood, but are in fact beech painted to simulate rosewood, a fashionable decorative effect of the Regency period.

The construction of globes

A pair of library globes combined the skills of the globe maker and the furniture maker. However, globes had been constructed for a very long time before they began to be mounted on stands. Very early examples, dating from antiquity, were carved in marble, and some Islamic celestial globes were engraved on hollow metal spheres. Most globes dating from the sixteenth to the early twentieth century were made from papier mâché covered with a layer of plaster, onto which 12 separate sections of engraved paper maps were pasted. In the late seventeenth century a thriving industry grew up, with the eighteenth and early nineteenth centuries being the high point of British globe making.

Overwhelming response

E very day a flood of letters arrives at the Roadshow's production office in Bristol. With occasional exceptions, they are all complimentary. Every correspondent receives a reply. Many people write to say "thank you" after visiting a Roadshow because they enjoyed the day. Others write to say that they own a piece that is almost identical to one shown on the programme. Not everyone is seeking a valuation – which, in any case, the BBC cannot provide – but may simply have a snippet of additional information, such as a family connection with an artist or potter. Many people spot a piece in the background, often an object that was used to dress the set, wanting to establish exactly what it is because they have one like it. Roadshow fans also write asking when the team will be visiting their area, while some suggest venues. The Roadshow is very much a part of people's lives, and by writing in viewers and visitors make a connection with the programme that is important to them and to the BBC.

The Roadshow has provided a rich vein of material for comedy writers, and as a familiar feature of modern life it is sure to be a source of merriment in the future. Apart from that, the programme is fun to make – for visitors, experts and crew alike – and it is hoped that this is evident to the eight million people who watch every Sunday.

Ex-presenter Hugh Scully (left) with the then executive producer Christopher Lewis, who holds the BAFTA award won by the *Antiques Roadshow*: the Lew Grade Award for a Significant and Popular Programme, 1995.

Producer's last word

Not long after assuming the reins, I was asked what it felt like to take on such a long-running and successful series as the *Antiques Roadshow*. I remember saying it must be akin to becoming the captain of a magnificent liner on which a dedicated group of fans have enjoyed popular cruises under an immensely professional crew for decades. Having stood on deck for what is now approaching my first year, I think the analogy was a good one. It is indeed a handsome vessel, the envy of many a fleet, but mine is also a bit of a scary responsibility, as you quickly realize just how easy it would be to knock our ship off course as you embark on what we hope will be another memorable tour. And my maiden voyage has proved quite an adventure.

Picture this scene. It's midsummer at an English country seat. Under the handsome frontage of Wilton House, near Salisbury, the Roadshow is poised to record another edition. This is the moment you hope months of planning has adequately prepared you for, as our team of experts stand by to meet the hundreds of people who've been patiently queuing since early morning. But at this event every eye is cast to the skies as a bruised and angry-looking storm approaches. True we have a marquee for shelter, but such is the noise as a gale starts to blow against the metal frame we quickly realize that recordings undercover won't really be audible. The only option is to hope the storm will blow through and that the resilience of all involved will see us through. Sadly conditions worsen and the only real shelter to be taken is on the narrow Palladian bridge that spans the river. At one point I count over 40 people huddled underneath its arches as a full outside-broadcast unit stoically continues recording at one end. It's worth noting that such was the appalling weather, the Hampton Court Flower Show was closed on the very same day, but the Roadshow carried on. At one point books expert Clive Farahar even had to throw himself bodily across a fragile and valuable manuscript to protect it from the onslaught. For the producer who'd taken the decision to record more outdoor programmes than ever before, (yes that was me) this proved quite a baptism in a year that saw many wet summer days!

And we've been challenged in other, even more unexpected ways. At the new National Trust star location, Tyntesfield, an overheating tea urn triggered the fire alarm that saw 15 fire engines roar up to the house during recording. Badgers chewed through our camera cables at Witley Court, blacking out our monitors when we rolled up to record the next morning, and at Victoria Baths in Manchester (my decision again) meant that we had to board over one and a half of the vast pools to accommodate the turnout. But, despite these blips, we've continued finding more exciting treasures that have turned into fascinating and, I hope, memorable television.

What's proved perhaps the most intriguing for me from my vantage point is a recognition of just how clever the original concept underpinning the Roadshow was, and still is today. In an era of TV that demands faster action, higher stakes, continued jeopardy and heightened anxiety over viewing figures, the *Antiques Roadshow* may appear a gentle and warmly familiar friend from quieter times, yet its power to hold and entertain large audiences is undiminished, because at its heart is a compelling formula: a blend of intrigue, great stories, remarkable characters and, underpinning it all, the game of "What's it worth?" That's a formula that many a "reality" show would give its right arm for. Long may it continue.

Simon Sle

index

ANTIQUES ROADSHOW

Lecture & Conference Services

A unique opportunity...

The Antiques Roadshow is a television phenomenon in Britain and abroad. Watched by millions for over twenty five years, the programme and its experts offer a compelling blend of culture and entertainment.

The Antiques Roadshow Lecture and Conference Service is unique. It is the only company to hold a licence from BBC Worldwide to use the Antiques Roadshow name in connection with the corporate and entertainment markets. With this, we can present the special qualities of the programme and feature the well-known Antiques Roadshow experts; experts who are outstanding specialists and experienced performers in their fields.

We have devised and presented entertainment or management training programmes based on art and antiques for clients including BT, Hilton Hotels, Jaguar Cars, Mercedes Benz, NADFAS, the National Trust, the NEC, Norwich Union, Radisson Cruise Lines, Rolls Royce Cars, the Rotary Club, Tesco, Toyota and J Walter Thompson. All events are tailor-made to your requirements and we create programmes which will engage small groups as well as large audiences during the day, after dinner or for a weekend.

For find out more look at our website **www.antiquesroadshow-lcs.com**
or contact us on **enquiries@antiquesroadshow-lcs.com**, or by post, fax or telephone
ARLCS, PO BOX 47, ABINGDON OX13 6XT, UK
TEL: **(+44) 01865 390942** • FAX: **(+44) 01865 390943**

HOMES
&ANTIQUES
MAGAZINE

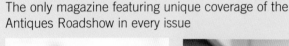

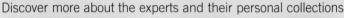

Acknowledgments

The editor would like to thank all who have helped him on this book including the experts and behind-the-scenes staff, who have been tolerent of his persistent demands on their time, singling out particularly Olwen Gillespie whose equilibrium he tried on many an occasion. Mary Carrol and William Wildblood of *Homes & Antiques*, without whose pictures the book would have been bleak, warrant special thanks, as does Simon Shaw, line editor of the *Roadshow* for his understanding and helpful comments. The editor apologises for his panics and thanks for their patience Anna Sanderson, Emily Asquith and Christine Keilty from Mitchell Beazley. Finally, thanks to his wife for her Job-like endurance as the book took its inevitable toll on his nerves and to the dedicated and speedy professionalism of the writer, Fiona Malcolm.

Picture credits

The publishers would like to thank all the photographers who have contributed to this book. The publishers apologise if any errors or omissions have been made and would be happy to make corrections in future editions.

Key t: top; m: middle; b: bottom; r: right; l:left; c: centre

David Battie: 21t; 26bl; 27; 32tr; 36; 37; 43; 54; 55; 58; 59bl, t; 60tr; 61br; 62; 63 all but bc; 68; 69; 70; 71tl; 72 br; 73t, bl; 74; 75b; 77b; 79t; 85 bl; 86 bl; 87bl;, 88; 89b

Clive Corless/Homes & Antiques Archive: 5; 11; 23; 26 except bl; 29; 32 all but tr; 35; 38; 41; 44; 47; 50; 53; 56; 59br; 60 all but tr; 61 all but br; 63 bc; 90; 91; 92t

BBC Archives: 6; 8/9; 10; 20; 21b

Mick Dunning: Title; 12; 13; 14; 15; 16; 17; 18/19; 22; 64; 65; 66-7; 73bl; 75t; 77 t; m, r, 79m, b; 80t, bl; 81; 82 t, m, bl; 83t, br; 84 all but br; 85 all but bl; 86t, br; 87 all but bl

Olwen Gillespie: 95 br; 118 b

Brian Hawkins: 92m, b

Bob Laughton: 40

Octopus Publishing Group/Tom Ridley: 24; 25; 28; 30; 31; 34; 39; 45; 51; 57; 71 tr, b; 72 l, tr; 76; 78; 80 br; 82 br; 83 bl; 89 t

Sebastian Stevens: 33; 42; 46; 48; 49; 52

City of Stoke on Trent Department of Leisure and Cultural Services. City Museum and Art Gallery/Photos courtesy of Potteries Museum and Art Gallery, Stoke-on-Trent: Half title

Lars Tharp: 73br; 84 br; 93 all but br

Endpapers, clockwise from top left: 83tr Ben Shilow; 84br Radio Times/Ken Pyne; 84t Bellworks/Steve Bell; 83c Private Eye/Berkin; 83tl Jonathan Pugh/The Times; 84bl Mirror Group Newspapers/Langdon; 83b Peter Knight/AUGUSTA Copyright cartoon by permission of Angus McGill and Dominic Poelsma; 84c The Spectator/Reproduced from The Spectator.

Course, this china would've been worth a lot
more had it not been damaged